Making Money with Donor Newsletters

The How-To Guide
To Extraordinary Results

Of Related Interest

How to Write Fundaising Materials that Raise More Money
By Tom Ahern, 187 pp., $24.95.

Whenever we're called upon to draft a solicitation letter or write copy for the website or, heaven forbid, pen long stretches of a proposal or case statement, we sit there ... and if we're lucky crank out serviceable prose. Few would call it sparkling. Even fewer are moved to write a check in response.

It won't be this way any longer for those who invest a few hours in *How to Write Fundraising Materials that Raise More Money*. Communicating with donors is the bedrock of all fundraising. And no book addresses this topic with such virtuosity.

Seeing Through a Donor's Eyes
By Tom Ahern, 167 pp., $24.95.

Successful donor newsletters, websites, annual reports, donor acquisition programs, email, direct mail, and, yes, capital campaigns too, all have one thing in common: behind each stands a well-reasoned, emotionally satisfying case for support.

Regularly reviewing your case is due diligence in a well-managed fundraising office. And it doesn't have to be a laborious project: answer a few questions and you're done.

Of course, if your office is launching a big-bucks campaign, the step-by-step process revealed in this book guarantees you'll tell a persuasive, sharply focused story, even when you have a hundred moving parts.

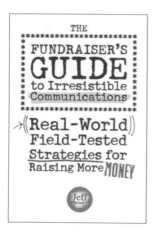

The Fundraiser's Guide to Irresistible Communications
By Jeff Brooks, 143 pp., $24.95.

Here it is: an easy-to-read and spritely book that reveals what really works in fundraising. Not academic theory or wishful thinking, but ways of communicating that are proven to motivate donors to give generously, wholeheartedly, and repeatedly.

Drawing from decades of in-the-trenches experience, Jeff Brooks, one of America's top fundraising writers, takes you on a step-by-step tour of the unique strategies, writing style, and design techniques of irresistible fundraising messages.

www.emersonandchurch.com

Tom Ahern

Making Money with Donor Newsletters

The How-To Guide
To Extraordinary Results

Foreword by Roger Craver

Emerson
& Church
PUBLISHERS

www.emersonandchurch.com

First printed in October 2013

10   9   8   7   6   5   4   3   2

Printed in the United States of America

This text is printed on acid-free paper.

Copies of this book are available from the publisher at discount when purchased in quantity for boards of directors or staff.

Emerson & Church, Publishers
15 Brook Street, Medfield, MA 02052
Tel. 508-359-0019 - Fax 508-359-2703
www.emersonandchurch.com

Library of Congress Cataloging-in-Publication Data
Ahern, Tom.

    Making money with donor newsletters : the how-to guide to extraordinary results / Tom Ahern.
        pages cm
    ISBN 978-1-889102-50-4 (pbk. : alk. paper)   1. Direct-mail fund raising.   2. Newsletters—Design.   3. Nonprofit organizations—Finance.   I. Title.
    HV41.2.A435 2013
    658.15′224   dc23
                                                                        2013030709

For Simone, who kissed me to life

Contents

Foreword

Too many fundraisers are spending too much time in search of the next and greatest new thing. Like hunting dogs ranging back and forth in pursuit of a fresh scent, they endlessly pursue some magic bullet that never seems to hit the fundraising mark.

Infatuation with social media—Facebook, Twitter, Instagram, you name it—is the latest manifestation of this elusive quest for the quick and easy pot of fundraising gold at the end of the high tech rainbow.

Search no more. The answer, 'the magic bullet,' is in fact staring us in the face. *Making Money with Donor Newsletters* rediscovers and reveals how, what, and why a 3,000 year-old technology—words and pictures on paper—when properly employed can unlock a treasure trove of contributions and donor loyalty most nonprofits only dream of.

It's time to rediscover the lowly donor newsletter. This low-tech ugly duckling hiding in plain sight amidst the rhinestone sparkle of over-hyped high tech tools can easily be transformed into a beautiful swan able to revolutionize your fundraising.

In brief, a properly prepared newsletter will add heaps to your bottom line...bring leaps of joy to your donors...and boost your organization's donor retention to new heights.

This book is long overdue. Donor acquisition costs are at an all-time high. Donor retention rates are at an all-time low. Why? Because a donor's giving behavior depends on the attitude of that donor towards your charity. Whether that attitude is positive or negative is determined by the actions your organization itself takes.

There's no action a fundraiser can take that is more essential or profitable than making certain the donor knows how important and wonderful she or he is. And there's no communications vehicle as powerfully suited for this task than the simple, well-written four-page paper newsletter. Not digital. Not slick. Not focused on the ego of the organization. It's not about you. It's all about the donor.

Perhaps you're wondering, "Is this book for me?" I promise, with complete confidence, that the practical, step-by-step approach taken by Tom Ahern will boost your communications skills—and results— quickly and dramatically.

If you're just beginning to spread your fundraising wings this book is perfect for you. You'll learn key principles you can apply immediately. Skills that will put you in good stead today and throughout your entire career.

If you're already a successful and accomplished fundraiser this book will help you better understand how to use the skills you already have to become even more effective.

Read and heed. Follow the clear and tested approaches outlined and you'll be amply rewarded. *Making Money with Donor Newsletters* will help you transform your current newsletter into a money machine —some charities that have followed this advice have improved income by 1000 percent! More importantly it will guide you in transforming your organization from a ho-hum 'corporate-focused' entity into a distinctive and thriving 'donor-focused' powerhouse.

Tom Ahern combines writing that is both fine and fun with insight and great wit. His is that rare practical experience that comes from decades as one of America's great fundraising communications experts. It's worth noting that Tom was successfully working on effective communications before the invention of the Internet, when a 'mobile device' was a briefcase, and 'software' was something found in the linens section of department stores.

It is Tom's deep and timeless experience, his wit and wisdom that make his insights and advice in this book so valuable. More than anyone I know he has brilliantly lifted the lowly donor newsletter to its rightful—yes, exalted—place as the essential building block in donor communications.

Making Money with Donor Newsletters is not a theoretical work. Every chapter is jam-packed with 'how to' illustrations and guidance. You'll discover that none of the skills required is difficult to master. If you can write a letter to your mother or your kid at camp you have within you the wherewithal to write a dynamite newsletter.

Let others cast out and about for the next "new, new thing" that glows in the dark and hypes its promises of a fundraising revolution. You're about to be treated to a remarkable rediscovery of an "old, old thing" that not only raises more money, but also builds more lasting donor loyalty and retention.

I wish you success and fun in this discovery.

Roger M. Craver
Chilmark, Massachusetts

Pep Talk and Promise

If you, as a fundraiser, are disappointed with your newsletter's results—as I suspect many organizations are—here's one thing I can promise you:

You could be doing much better.

Success is within every nonprofit's grasp. That promise is based on years of experience with all sorts of charities of all sizes.

There's just one little obstacle

Doing a successful donor newsletter is easy.

There are models to copy inside this book. None of the skills required are difficult to master, including the writing. If you can write a chatty letter to your mother, you can write a donor newsletter.

There's only one hard thing that stands in your way.

You.

We're all conservative in some sense. We hate to change the way we do things.

But . . . . You have to change what you've been doing. You can't get better results by doing the same old thing.

The old newsletter? It'll have defenders.

The things you'll learn in this book are things you don't yet know. I didn't know them either, when I started my "journey into the jungle of donor newsletters" back in 1999, in Miami, at an NSFRE (now AFP) conference. That was where I encountered the Domain Formula.

I was suspicious: "Will these rules work in our special case?"[1]

But my clients took the risk. And reaped surprising, even shocking, benefits. One client now receives a half million dollars annually in newsletter-generated gifts from a 4-time-a-year mailing to about 10,000 donors.

---

1 Later I learned there *are* no special cases. At one level, all charities are the same, as far as donors are concerned.

What makes this *truly* amazing is: *newsletters aren't about revenue.* They're not little machines for manufacturing additional gifts.

Actually, donor newsletters are about retention. They're meant to help retain donors longer by reporting on the impact their gifts have had on the world. Any gifts that arrive as a result are pure gravy and not part of the business plan.

Of course, don't shun the metric, either. "How do you know your donor newsletter is working beautifully?" It'll bring in a significant number of additional gifts.

PART I

The Breakthrough

CHAPTER 1

The Secret to Success

Only a certain type of newsletter keeps donors inspired and attracts lots of gifts. Most nonprofit newsletters do neither of those things. Yours can be one of the few that does.

Here's the secret. Profitable charity newsletters are *not* about how wonderful your organization is. Charity newsletters become profitable when they focus on how wonderful the *donor* is. Your mantra:

- It's not about you. It's about the donor.

- Not about you. About the donor.

- Not you. The donor.

This is easy stuff.

Back in the 1990s, as a senior creative at Seattle's Domain Group, Jeff Brooks helped develop the newsletter formula you'll learn about in this book. In 2012, with almost two decades of newsletter experience under his belt, Jeff observed, "The reason so many nonprofit newsletters are just big money-sinks is this: Their purpose is to educate their donors about how effective the organization is. The money-making donor-focused newsletter has a different purpose: *To remind the donor what an incredible difference she makes.*"

As I say, this is easy stuff.

CHAPTER 2

Delivering Joy: The True Purpose of a Donor Newsletter

What is a donor newsletter really for?

Aside from delivering news, it has one other primary purpose: to bring joy into the homes of your supporters.

Joy is the point. "Newsletter" is just the name of the container.

That's what I think, anyway. And I think that because I've seen how a focus on joy can work wonders to unlock vast new reserves of caring and generosity.

Most charity newsletters miss that point. They're not about the donor. They're about the organization. And they try to sell stuff, which is a mistake.

Your donor newsletter is *not* for selling stuff like planned gifts. A sales-oriented newsletter is inauthentic and unwelcome. It won't pass the smell test with donors.

Sales are a by-product. The sales you make through your newsletter will be made on the coattails of joy. Keep your priorities straight: joy first, everything else second.

The joy roll

What kinds of joy am I talking about? Pretend you're a donor. The latest issue of the newsletter has just arrived. As you look and read, do you immediately experience . . .

- The joy of learning what a wonderful person you are

- The joy of knowing you're a loving person

- The joy of knowing you're a contributor to society

- The joy of seeing yourself as a problem solver

- The joy of being a member of something pretty special

- The joy of seeing your values affirmed and acted upon

- The joy of making your world a better place

- The joy of feeling you've performed your duty to your fellows

Yes? No? Not sure? Read on.

Operation Homefront's full-color newsletter brings joy to its donors . . . and they respond generously. The Heart of the Mission newsletter, featured on the next two pages, is another top-dollar performer.

Heart *of the* Mission

JUNE 2013

feels like HOME

You've given this mom and her son hope

INSIDE
Find out why WSMV's Lisa Spencer loves the Mission

The blessing of volunteering is a two-way street

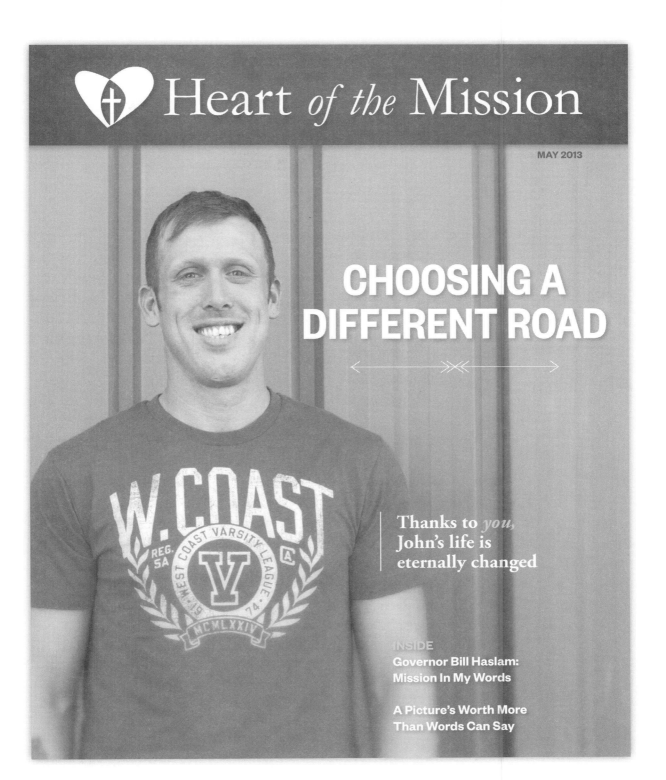

Heart *of the* **Mission**

MAY 2013

CHOOSING A DIFFERENT ROAD

Thanks to *you,* John's life is eternally changed

INSIDE
Governor Bill Haslam: Mission In My Words

A Picture's Worth More Than Words Can Say

Heart of the Mission delivers joy to the donor on every cover: "Thanks to you, John's life is eternally changed." Donors respond richly. Average gift prompted by the newsletter: $77. Record response so far for one issue: $308,000 in contributions ($220,000 is more typical). This full-color, 8-page newsletter accounts for $2 million worth of charitable income a year for Nashville Rescue Mission. Writer/editor: Michelle Sanders Brinson; designer: Jessica Mason. (*Reprinted with Permission*)

CHAPTER 3

A Word on Donor (Dis)loyalty

How "loyal" is the average donor?

Not very, it seems.

"In many large national programs fueled by direct mail," arch-guru Mal Warwick observed, "no more than 25–35 percent of newly acquired donors ever give so much as a second gift." In 2013, Blackbaud's Chief Scientist, Chuck Longfield, reported exactly the same depressing results: 70 percent of newly-acquired donors leave by the end of the first year.

It's relatively easy to get a first gift. It's consistently hard to get a second gift.

I have more bad news, about attitudes toward charity generally.

"The average American believes that it's reasonable for charities to spend 23 cents out of every dollar raised on fundraising and administrative costs," Grey Matter Research reported in 2012. Don't break out the champagne, though. "Unfortunately, the average American also believes that charities actually spend 37 cents out of every dollar raised on such costs."

"Public confidence in charities remains at contemporary lows," the Brookings Institution reported in 2002. In 2008, Brookings revisited the issue and found that public confidence had eroded still more: 70 percent of Americans said that charities waste "a great deal" or "fair amount" of money, a record high for a very negative indicator.

And yet donors still give. Imagine what they might give if they actually trusted us?

Be aware: charities are guilty until proven innocent

Part of the problem is the name, I suppose. We call ourselves "non-profits." And what does that label say subliminally to the layperson? That we really don't care about money.

UK researchers once asked donors to guess, "What percentage of your gift does your favorite charity spend on its fundraising activities, rather than on programs?"

Prepare yourself. Donors believed that most of their gift—65 percent—was plowed back into fundraising and related overhead, leaving only a small share—a mere 35 percent—for changing the world. And yet they still gave.

You're protesting: *"That's so unfair! We pour almost everything we're given directly into programs. We spend as little as possible on fundraising."*

You know that. I know that. But your donors *don't* know that. You have to remind them of your organization's dedication to transparency, accountability, and financial health, in every issue of your newsletter.

Donor loyalty depends to some degree on trust. And donors in general aren't that trusting. They assume charities aren't very efficient or business-minded. That assumption has a chilling effect.

Bruce Campbell, a pioneering researcher into donor attitudes and behavior, found that "information regarding how finances are used" was among donors' top concerns. They wonder: "Did you spend my money on paper clips and business lunches? Or did you really use my gift to change the world?"

Don't leave your donors guessing on this point. They *will* guess wrong . . . and not in your favor.

CHAPTER 4

Common Obstacles

Let's tear down some barriers.

- **We did a newsletter before. It didn't work for us.** This conclusion implies that some organizations just aren't "good newsletter material," when in fact most newsletters fail for a few obvious reasons which you'll learn about in this book.

- **I'm a fundraiser, not a journalist.** You don't have to be a great writer to create a great charity newsletter. Honest: this book is NOT about turning you into a journalist. You have better ways to spend your time.

  Paradoxically enough, your newsletter isn't *about* getting people to read your articles. Your newsletter, as I stressed in the previous chapter, is *actually* about delivering joy to your donors repeatedly . . . and as fast as possible. You can swiftly accomplish that profitable feat in a handful of headlines. Why? Because research shows that most "readers" never venture far past the headlines, even in Pulitzer-winning newspapers.

  Mothball your "writer's block" anxieties. You don't need to write exquisite articles. You *will* need to learn how to write a competent headline. But that's about it. And it's an easily acquired skill.

- **I have other priorities.** I hear you: my to-do list always outpaces my workday. So the question becomes (especially in a small or one-person fundraising shop): *Is a newsletter worth making time for?* Should it be a top priority or an also-ran?

  Well, that depends. If your organization believes (as I do, because I've seen the proof repeatedly) that donor-centricity is the surest route to increased income and retention, then you *need* a tool to help you nurture relationships with *all* your donors—not just those lucky few you can reach one on one. The proper tool for mass cultivation is the donor newsletter. It affords you an efficient way to speak to your entire donor base on a regular basis.

- **I don't have any stories.** "There are eight million stories in the Naked City. This has been one of them," the narrator intoned at the close of each episode. Naked City was one of the first TV crime dramas, set in New York City. They knew they'd never run out of stories.

  You have that kind of abundance at your fingertips, too. You just have to look for it—or, even better, train your colleagues to search it out for you.

  Collect stories all the time. At Health Care for the Homeless (Baltimore), the director of development makes a practice of regularly trolling the front-line staff for true-life stories. The fundraiser also educated the social workers there about the financial good it does the agency to have great stories to tell. As a result, social workers have become eager "story gatherers." You're not asking them to write up polished 500-word summaries, either. You're asking them to pop 50 rough words into an email.

- **I'm not a designer.** You don't have to be. Even the most graphically challenged can send out a simple (yet soul-satisfying) "newsy-letter" to donors. It's nothing more than a Word document. Trust me: if you can write *any* kind of letter (to your son at camp?), then you can write a successful newsy-letter. *See Chapter 43 in the Table of Contents.*

- **I can't justify it to my boss.** Look: the financial hurdle for newsletters is really low. If you break even—if you bring in enough gifts to cover your postage and printing—then you're already beating the odds. Donor newsletters aren't about current income, after all (though they *can* produce miracles in that department). Donor newsletters are about retaining donors for the long haul.

CHAPTER 5

Where the Real Money is (Hint: Not in Acquisition)

Why do nonprofits using direct mail to acquire new donors commonly spend $2 in printing, postage, list rental and other costs to raise just $1 in giving?

Because the real money comes later. If you retain those new donors, their subsequent gifts, including the potential for a charitable bequest—the ultimate gift—make that "spend $2 to make $1" initial investment well worth the risk.

There's just one problem.

According to experts in several countries, nonprofits generally don't hold on to many first-time donors.

We saw Chuck Longfield's 2013 report from Blackbaud: 70 percent of first-time donors are gone within a year.

In their 2010 book, *Fundraising Principles and Practice*, researchers Adrian Sargeant and Jen Shang found that a typical UK charity "will lose 50 percent of its cash (that is, annual) donors between the first and second donation, and up to 30 percent annually thereafter." Recent US data, they point out, looked even worse, "with attrition rates in initial cash giving being reported at a mean of 74 percent."

At the 2011 IFC Congress in The Netherlands, globe-trotting consultant Tony Elischer said that over 60 percent of donors give just once, a retention rate he called "shameful."

The percentages vary. But the lesson is clear: as an industry, nonprofits are poor at donor retention.

The price of poor donor retention

According to Harvey McKinnon, founder of a top Canadian fundraising firm, the biggest gift a donor ever makes is usually around the

6th to 8th gift. But as we've just seen, most donors won't stick with you that long.

Being very, very good at your mission guarantees you nothing by the way, re: the retention of individual donors.

I'm thinking of a specific charity. It was founded in the 1970s. And it has grown and grown because it's uniquely effective at helping poor families in crisis. Government, corporate, and foundation funders love it. But what about its individual donors?

Alas: 72 percent of its first-time, individual donors do NOT make a second gift, the in-house data reveals. By year two, 94 percent of its newly acquired donors have disappeared, never to be seen again. Those are recent, real numbers.

Are those numbers a shame, as Mr. Elischer has it? Well, they could be, if they were irreversible. But they aren't. You CAN hold onto more donors, if you try. Actually, today's poor performance in retention is a huge opportunity for additional charitable income, just waiting to be exploited. "All" you have to do is reverse your losses by keeping your donors longer.

Better retention is the cheapest money you'll ever raise

Let's look at what a modest improvement in retention can do for your bottom line.

"Typically," writes Prof. Sargeant in his book, *Tiny Essentials of Donor Loyalty*, "a 10 percent improvement in the level of loyalty . . . increases the lifetime value of the fundraising database by around 50 percent."

I have recent data from Australia, from Pareto, the country's largest direct mail fundraising firm. For one of Pareto's clients, in the first year, the Return on Investment (ROI) for a new donor was 88 cents for every dollar spent to acquire that donor. In other words, the charity lost money on acquisition, which is not at all uncommon.

But hold onto those donors and time will heal the financial wound. By year five, the ROI for that same lot of donors had risen to $3.83 per dollar spent. By year five, the donors who were still with the charity were returning almost four times what the charity spent to solicit them.

So the question becomes: "How do we improve retention?"

Newsletters are part of the answer.

Not just any old kind of newsletter, mind you.

To be effective at retention, your organization's newsletter must anticipate and fulfill the psychological cravings of its target audience: the donors.

Don't let that intimidate you, though. It's easy enough to give donors exactly what they need and want in a newsletter, as you will soon discover. In fact, it's fun!

Joan Flanagan is the author of *Successful Fundraising*. She's taught legions of novice fundraisers the basics. Joan has said, "All the knowledge about fundraising can be summed up in ten words: ask 'em, thank 'em, ask 'em again, thank 'em again."

I'd like to add one more item to Joan's virtuous circle: the report to donors, delivered via print and emailed newsletters (different beasts, as you'll learn).

Jim Shapiro and Steven Screen, Seattle-based co-founders of Better Fundraising for All, teach a simple communications system called Ask, Thank, Report, Repeat. "It's a rhythm that increases revenue and builds relationships with your donors."

I totally concur.

CHAPTER 6

Better Customer Service Equals Increased Donor Loyalty

Fundraising is a kind of sales and marketing.

And to succeed in sales and marketing, you have to know: *Who is my customer?* Is it your boss? Is it the board? Is it "the world" or "the community"?

None of the above.

In fundraising, the real—the *only*—customer is your donor . . . not the organization you work for, nor the world you serve.

Why?

Because the money you're trying to raise comes from donors. Not from your organization. In marketing, your customer is the person who hands over the cash; hence, your donor is your customer.

Treating your donor as a customer whom you wish to please is the secret behind improved satisfaction and the incredible leaps in income that happen thereafter, as unprecedented amounts of new charitable revenue flow in and donor retention strengthens.

No one knows more about keeping notoriously fickle donors satisfied and generous than researcher Adrian Sargeant, Ph.D., a Brit academic who was named the first Robert F. Hartsook Professor of Fundraising at Indiana University.

He found seven things improve donor loyalty. When . . .

- You deliver good service to your donors

- Your donors are aware of consequences

- Your donors trust you

- Your donors share your beliefs

- You achieve a personal relationship with your donors

- Your donors are learning (they're on a journey)

- You offer multiple engagements

A donor newsletter can help you make gains with all seven of these "loyalty inducing" factors. Let's look at just one: service quality.

What is "service quality"? Rare, unfortunately.

Adrian Sargeant has a warning. "To paraphrase one of the great marketing thinkers, [Harvard Business School professor] Theodore Levitt famously noted that, in the service context, people generally only know what they want when they don't get it."

It's even more complicated. Professor Levitt's comment assumes that people have had a negative experience so clear and strong that it rose to their notice. As in, "Waiter, this coffee is cold."

But I suspect where donors are concerned, negative experiences are quite frequent but often *unnoticed* on the conscious level.

I'll use my own experience as a donor as an example.

Our household gives to at least 20 charities a year. Yet, I can think of just three that consistently deliver good service to us and other donors. What do they do? In all the communications . . . .

- They ask well. They thank well. And they report well.

- They make me feel important and useful as a donor.

- They make me feel smart for having chosen them.

- They bring joy to my home.

- They make me part of a good fight worth winning.

- They give me a way to express my values and hopes.

Please note: I get nothing but feelings from them. No tangibles like tote bags. No discounted tickets. But you know what? Good feelings are worth far more to me than stuff. I can buy my own stuff, thank you. What I can't buy is what only you, my charity, can give me: feelings of being needed, of being welcomed, of being important to the outcome.

When I feel good about myself thanks to "my" charities, then I feel good about them as well. Which is the source of better retention: fundraising's customers (i.e., your donors) are happy with you.

What about the other, you're probably wondering, the charities that don't make me feel good about myself?

Well, that's the thing with customer (i.e., donor) service. It's pass/fail. There are no nuances.

And most of the charities we give to fail us in their communications. We occasionally still give to them despite their lousy donor communications, because of what they do. But the links are loose. We drop them without a second thought. And we give them nominal gifts. Our big gifts go to the charities that make us happy.

Getting all emotional (for fun and profit)

Let's do a thought experiment. Get a pen and a pad of paper. Put yourself in your average donor's shoes for a moment and try to answer the following three questions (take all the time you want):

- What would you love to receive after you've made your very first gift?

- What would delight you had you made a second gift?

- And, if you'd made a third gift, what would surprise you so much you'd say to yourself, "Well, my word, isn't that amazing! Round up the kids: I want them to see this!"

Before you rush to answer, first note the verbs: *love, delight, surprise*. Nothing rational there. Just heartstrings; trying, *hoping* to be plucked. I can't make donor newsletters any simpler than this:

- They express love for the donor.

- They bring joy to the donor.

- They surprise the donor.

If you do all three of these things . . . you *will* have satisfied donors. If you rigorously judge every item in your newsletter against just three basic emotional standards (*does the item express love? does it bring*

THE
Your Hospital.
Your Health.
CAMPAIGN

Vol. 1: Issue 7   November 1, 2012

$1.25 Million Gift Brings Campaign to Over $10.5 Million

The "Your Hospital. Your Health." campaign has now topped $10.5 million thanks to a very generous $1.25 million gift from the Jeff and Jennie Sidwell family.

Genesis HealthCare System will create the **Jeff and Jennie Sidwell Family Women's and Children's Center** as part of the new Genesis medical center.

The Sidwell Family

"Creating a new medical center is central to the continued growth of our area and the health and well-being of our neighbors and community. Our family is pleased to be able to make this gift. We encourage everyone to be a part of this campaign and support the vision of quality health care in our region," said Jeff Sidwell.

"So many wonderful people are putting in a lot of effort in this campaign and making incredible gifts to see this vision of a new medical center become a reality. There are no words sufficient to thank Jeff and Jennie for their support of this campaign, our mission, and our community," said Matthew Perry, CEO of Genesis HealthCare System.

The Sidwell Family's gift brings the "Your Hospital. Your Health." campaign to more than $10.5 million.

"It's been amazing to meet, almost every day, with people in our region who want to know what role they can play in this campaign. We've received gifts ranging from a few dollars to over a million dollars. Each and every gift is important. Donors are investing in our community and the future of this region. The more support we have, the more successful we'll be in making this dream a reality," said Paul McClelland, Executive Director of the Genesis HealthCare Foundation.

Planning for the New Medical Center Continues

Designing a new medical center and planning the construction process is a huge undertaking. It takes many months, often even years, to put all the pieces together.

"Since the new medical center will include a new pavilion, as well as a renovation of the existing Bethesda Hospital, the planning is even more intense. Things have to be done in a specific order to keep the hospital functioning with a high quality experience for our patients," said Matthew Perry.

Hospital leaders are working on everything from the construction timetable, financing, floor plans and the order in which departments will be moved to make construction as efficient as possible.

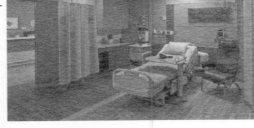

"We have excellent architects, designers and a top-rated national construction firm all working together to make the project economical and effective in both the short- and long-term," said Paul Masterson, Genesis' Chief Financial Officer.

More detailed plans will be released in early 2013, with construction tentatively scheduled to start in spring of 2013 and be completed in 2015.

Anonymous $250,000 Gift Adds Momentum

A local donor, who wishes to remain anonymous, recently made a $250,000 gift to the "Your Hospital. Your Health." capital campaign.

"This campaign is supporting one of the most important events in the history of our area. It's clear from the extraordinary levels of giving, both publicly and anonymously, that people see the need and benefit of a new medical center. Our community will become even more excited as design plans are revealed and construction starts," said Paul McClelland.

GENESIS HEALTHCARE
FOUNDATION
genesishcs.org/foundation
1135 Maple Ave. Zanesville, OH
(740) 454-5052

Page 2

Paul McClelland
pmcclelland@genesishcs.org

"Take your donors on a journey" is one of Adrian Sargeant's principles of donor loyalty. Executive director Paul McClelland at the Genesis HealthCare Foundation, Zanesville, OH, kept donors up to date on the progress of an important capital campaign with a special newsletter. *(Reprinted with Permission)*

joy? does it surprise?) . . . your donors will love you back intensely (i.e., send in more and bigger gifts).

We desperately want *satisfied* donors . . . for an obvious reason: because *satisfied* donors continue giving, just as *satisfied* customers continue buying.

Have *you* ever asked?

I was at a big recent AFP conference. And this was quite a moment.

Adrian Sargeant had just finished explaining to a room full of fundraisers how marketers depend on satisfaction surveys to sell more stuff.

Frequent little surveys, he'd said, provide the feedback necessary to refine products, improve services, and ensure a satisfying "customer experience."

Then he stepped out from behind the podium. He swept his arms wide and asked, "How many organizations in this room have ever conducted a donor satisfaction survey? How many of you have asked your donors how much they enjoy being your donor?"

There were maybe 150 attendees, standing room only.

Not a single hand went up.

Thus neatly making his point: fundraising is a form of marketing . . . and *yet* most fundraisers don't use marketing's most common and revealing tool, the satisfaction survey.

In his *Tiny Essentials* book, Dr. Sargeant observes, "We seem to be forever playing catch-up in the fundraising profession with lessons learned many years before in the commercial sector. Corporates have known for over 30 years that the single biggest driver of customer loyalty is their satisfaction with the quality of service provided."

CHAPTER 7

The Domain Formula

How did the Domain Group turn the common charity newsletter from a bit player into a money-making star?

By taking nothing for granted. Domain's original research revealed:

- Self-mailed newsletters produced lousy results. They'll save you money upfront . . . and lose you money on the backend, for the most part.

- A charity newsletter is *not* a PR tool. It's a reporting device. It has to do just one thing to be effective: show how your donors are changing the world.

- A good charity newsletter can make overflowing buckets of money.

Domain developed a simple and reliable formula:

- **Send four pages, in a standard format.** In the U.S. and Canada, the standard single-page format measures 8.5 x 11 inches. In the UK and other Commonwealth nations, the standard single-page format is taller and narrower: the A4. Whatever; it's just rectangles. What *is* important is this: you don't have to send your donors a big, thick production. Four pages of trenchant copy is fine. Sufficient. Enough. They'll reward you for being blessedly brief.

- **Full-color is fine.** Charities, especially those serving the poor, are right to wonder: "Will our donors think we're wasting money if we print in full color?" Domain's research found it didn't matter, *all else being equal.* Now, that said, I know a food bank that switched from two-color to full-color in 2013—only to see giving to their newsletter fall by half. Their last two-color issue made about $50,000 in gifts, which had been their average return for years.

The new full-color issue made just $25,000. Was it full-color alone that killed giving? I doubt it. I suspect more damage was done because the first issue of the full-color newsletter didn't emphasize need well enough. It was too sunny and upbeat, so donors felt they weren't needed.

- **Do NOT send a self-mailer. Send the newsletter in an envelope instead.** This is the one that trips up many charities. They want to save money on their newsletter, which they typically view as an expense with little-to-no measurable return on investment (ROI). The cheapest way to mail a newsletter is to shun the added expense of an envelope and use a "self-mailing" format instead. That's usually a mistake. Repeated tests by Domain conclusively showed that self-mailers didn't, for the most part, produce great results. Gifts didn't roll in. The same newsletter in an envelope, on the other hand, could produce lots of gifts. Why the difference? The best guess at Domain was that self-mailed newsletters had "low perceived value," to use marketing jargon. Which is one way of saying that they mostly just got tossed in the trash unread.

- **On your newsletter's envelope, run a small amount of teaser copy** that says something like, *Dear wonderful human being, the latest issue of your donor newsletter enclosed.* (Or for certain specialized audiences: *The latest issue of your donor newsletter lies coiled inside like a cobra!*) A teaser that tells recipients "this is not another request for money" will increase your opening rate.

- **Send your newsletter exclusively to current donors.** Nonprofits have all sorts of formulas for mailing newsletters. Some send *only* to donors who make gifts above a certain level. Generally, this is a self-defeating policy, since loyal $10 annual donors are actually superb candidates for making charitable bequests, studies show. Some send to *everyone* including the mayor's office, every foundation they've ever met, plus your Crazy Aunt Nellie—just on general principles. "Couldn't hurt, right?" The shotgun approach is costly, though. Domain found that, for highest ROI, you should ONLY mail to current donors. Simple.

- **Include a reply envelope and a reply device.** Or an all-in-one reply envelope with integrated device. Does not matter. The envelope/device is there (1) to reinforce the idea that you need gifts; and (2) to give responsive donors a convenient way to return a gift check.

- **Mail "as often as possible."** Success is no accident; it's built step by step. If one of your newsletters produces an eyebrow-lifting amount of donor revenue, then double the frequency of the newsletter. If it continues to produce large amounts of income, then double your frequency again. A charity that has a winning newsletter could probably send it monthly and make disgraceful amounts of money with every issue. But let's be honest. Most charities aren't ready for that kind of full-court press. Take baby steps. If you're sending your newsletter just once a year, that's an annual report. A three-times-a-year printed newsletter is subsistence living. A quarterly printed newsletter is probably the true bare minimum.

- **Focus on accomplishment reporting.** "Accomplishment reporting" was Domain's term for "telling your donors the good things you did with their money." *Accomplishment reporting* is what your donors need to hear—in fact, what they *crave* hearing. Skip this, and your newsletter will fail: a one-step checklist.

What Jeff learned later

In 2012, Jeff Brooks sent me a note mentioning a few additional things he'd learned in the years since. In his own words:

- Fewer than four pages hasn't done well. When we've tested a single-sheet newsletter (8.5 x 11 or 8.5 x 14 inches) it has meaningfully underperformed a typical 4-page format. Cheaper, but the loss in revenue more than undercuts the production savings.

- A different format that has done well is this: four pages plus a 3-inch "flap." The entire form is 11 x 20 instead of 11 x 17 inches; the flap folds in over page 3. Allows for a little more content, and the cost difference is very little.

- Full color. When tested against two-color, four-color usually at least pays for itself. Full color seems to have the most positive impact for larger national organizations. It's worth testing, but not an automatic winner for everyone. (The cost difference between 2 and 4 color has shrunk; very often nowadays 2-color printing is done on 4-color presses; adding the other two colors adds very little expense.)

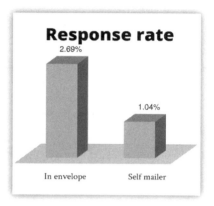

Data supplied by Jeff Brooks, June 2013

- Reply device printed in the newsletter as well as on the reply envelope. This usually gives a meaningful boost to response. Organizations get very few of these printed reply devices back, but they seem to drive more people to the separate RD in the envelope.

- "Newsletter enclosed" is the best teaser.

- You CAN ask in a newsletter. The newsletters that have appeals built into them, such as a lead story about some problem or opportunity that needs donor support, get the strongest response.

- Newsletters aren't equally effective for all organizations. They work better for local orgs than national ones. They generally work better for religious groups than non-religious. Organizations that have had newsletters for a while can usually improve response to newsletters and add more issues to the calendar. If you have no newsletter now, do 3 or 4 in the coming year. If they work, add more issues each year.

- Thirteen seems to be too many. We had a client that did a newsletter every month, and newsletters generally did better than appeal letters. So we added a 13th issue (in place of an appeal in the thick of the year-end season). That 13th did worse than most appeals.

- Try a personalized newsletter. Use lasering or digital printing to get the donor's name into headlines and other content. This works well, and pays for itself (though we have the feeling that it would get less effective if used a lot). Imagine the power of this headline: "Mr. and Mrs. Example helped hungry people this summer!"

Stand in awe

Let's give the last word to Jeff Schreifels, another Domain alumnus. He wrote me in 2012, about a client of his: "They too embraced the 'Domain formula' about eight years ago. They have 350,000 donors. They send 12 donor-focused newsletters per year, along with 12 to

13 appeal letters and each newsletter brings in over $1 million in revenue! I'm not kidding. The newsletter actually brings in more revenue than their appeals. Those newsletters consistently bring in more than a 4.5 to 5 to 1 ROI. Never have seen anything like it."

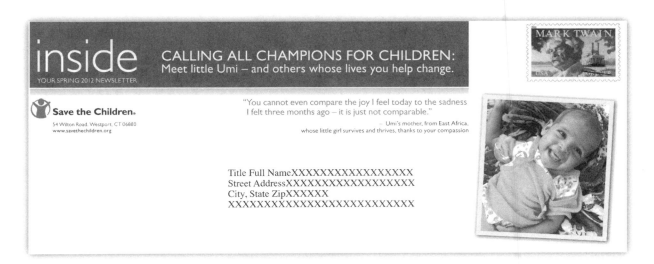

Save the Children's donor newsletter was built strictly to the Domain Formula, including the outbound envelope. It has been an enormous financial success. It replaced two earlier and unprofitable newsletters. (*Reprinted with Permission*)

CHAPTER 8

The "Gillette Miracle": How a Hospital Foundation Increased Giving to its Newsletter by 1,000%

I gave a workshop on newsletters.

People from Gillette Children's Specialty Healthcare in St. Paul, Minnesota attended. Their donor newsletter, mailed quarterly to 20,000 people at that point, racked up an annual net loss of $40,000. Was there a better way, they wondered?

Something amazing happened post-workshop: giving to Gillette's newsletter increased 1,000 percent (not a misprint), after a few changes.

The *old* way, the foundation received about $5,000 in gifts per issue.

The *new* way, the foundation received about $50,000 in gifts per issue.

OMG.

What changed

Exactly which details did Gillette choose to change in its newsletter? Here's the short list:

- **They made the donor the obvious hero.** Gillette pushed donor-centricity to an extreme I'd never encountered before. They thanked the donor copiously and obviously, in the big type (i.e., the headlines). They gave the donor credit without stint.

- **They switched from rational content to emotional content**, from coverage of technology and skills (the stuff that naturally fascinated the staff and defined the hospital's brand) to stories about kids getting better (the primary thing donors care about).

Please note: Gillette still gets to talk plenty about its amazing medicine, but the medicine plays a supporting role in a dramatic story about a child's recovery.

- **They made it personal.** The most powerful word in marketing, the word "you," never took top billing in the old version (if it appeared at all). In the new version, the word "you" is used with gusto, especially in high visibility locations like headlines. It has become the pronoun of choice.

- **They made it shorter.** The old newsletter was 8 pages long and text heavy. Now it's 4 pages long. Gillette also trimmed its articles. Lead articles used to average 1,200 words. Now they average 500 words.

- **It had been a self-mailer.** Now it's sent in a special envelope that says, in effect, "Your donor newsletter is enclosed. Thank you for your support!"

- **They went to full-color throughout.** The new design is much looser and fun. It crackles with visual energy and joy. It replaces an older design treatment that was mostly two-color and a bit dowdy.

By the way, despite enhancements like mailing the newsletter in an envelope bearing a live stamp along with a personalized cover letter and reply device, the new version, at half the length, cost no more than the old version.

In September 2009, Gillette's Angela Lindell and Andrew Olsen, CFRE, both key players in the makeover, published a frank, detailed article (you can Google it) about their newsletter's transformation. It appeared in the *Direct Marketing Association Journal*. The title: "Cutting Your Print Newsletter? Think Again! How We Transformed Ours Into a Moneymaker."

"A thorough review of [the old newsletter] quickly revealed a fundamental problem. We were telling the stories that made our organization look important—not the stories that made our donors feel important. We helped children walk. We opened new clinics. We conducted successful fundraising programs. We did amazing things! But all of our incredible accomplishments left the reader with a nagging question: 'If you're doing so great, why do you need me?'"

Angela and Andrew's article distilled their magic down to just three "simple—but incredibly important—things" that donors must hear from a newsletter:

- **"You matter."** Show your donors they're essential to your mission. Reframe your accomplishments as their accomplishments. ("Because of You, Douglas Can Visit an Imaging Center Without Crying!")

- **"You have invested wisely."** Prove that your organization is worthy of an investment.

- **"We still need you!"** Share new needs, opportunities and goals. Even when telling an amazing success story, leave your donors craving another interaction with you. ("Help Us Change More Lives.")

Gillette Children's
Specialty Healthcare

A CHILDREN'S MIRACLE
NETWORK AFFILIATE

Bringing You Closer to
the Lives You Help Change

Connections

Fall 2008 • Volume 1 • Number 1

Zawadi Says, "Thank You!"

You Helped a Tanzanian Girl Stand Tall on Her Own Two Feet

To meet Zawadi Rajabu, 6, is to experience gratitude through the eyes of a child. She greets you with a warm hug, a bright smile, and an emphatic, "Thank you!" Before you can grasp why you deserve such adoration, you catch a mischievous glint in her eye. "No catch me!" she taunts, running in the opposite direction. Another game of tag has begun, and — just like that — *you're it.*

It's an idyllic scene, but Zawadi's story doesn't begin here. Before she could even dream of chasing about in sparkly sneakers, Zawadi needed feet on which to stand.

Her Community Believed She Was Cursed
Zawadi was born with two clubfeet in an impoverished village outside Arusha, Tanzania. Her community saw the disability as a curse, and local children threw stones at her.

Zawadi's father abandoned the family the day she was born, leaving her mother to care for three children alone. "Zawadi would have no future if something happened to me," says Zawadi's mother, Sofia, through an interpreter.

Few Could Help Her
Zawadi's fate changed when missionaries Tom and Polly Wiley spotted her. "She had huge brown eyes and a penetrating look," Tom Wiley recalls. "We knew we had to help her."

The Wileys discovered that Zawadi's case was too severe for treatment in Tanzania. She needed a surgeon trained in the Ilizarov method — a complex technique for reshaping bones, developed by Gavriil Ilizarov, M.D., in a remote Siberian hospital. It was a tall order, to be sure.

But a Google search quickly uncovered one of the few surgeons in the world who could help Zawadi: Mark Dahl, M.D., pediatric orthopaedic surgeon at Gillette Children's Specialty Healthcare. In fact, Dahl trained in Siberia with Ilizarov himself.

"My Daughter Has a Future!"
Within weeks, Zawadi flew to St. Paul for a treatment that Dahl had performed thousands of times, but on only a few children with Zawadi's condition. During a five-hour surgery, Dahl

Zawadi continued on Page 4

Because of You!

Zawadi wears sparkly new shoes
Page 1

Douglas can visit an imaging center without crying
Page 2

Katie's memory continues to inspire
Page 2

Grace can say, "I love you!"
Page 3

Without treatment in Tanzania, Zawadi (right) learned to walk on the rough calluses that formed where her feet should be.

But today, Zawadi (above) is shopping for her first pairs of shoes! Wal-Mart helped her find shoes that fit around her braces, which will keep her feet straight while she grows.

Illustrated: the four-page inaugural issue of Gillette Children's "donor-centered" newsletter. When this donor-adoring newsletter first landed in homes, charitable giving in response jumped 1,000 percent immediately and has remained extraordinary ever since. *(Reprinted with Permission)*

A Word From Our President . . .
Margaret Perryman

What's So Special About Specialty Care?

"Specialty health care" is a phrase we often use at Gillette, but what does it really mean? You might say that we focus on the hard stuff — some of the most uncommon diagnoses and complex treatments in medicine. Just read the real-life stories in this issue of *Connections*, and I think you'll understand what's so special about the care we provide.

For example: *Who has one of the world's few surgeons skilled in the rare orthopaedic treatments pioneered by Gavriil Ilizarov in Siberia?* We do.

Who has the technology to help a child break free from silence, expressing something as simple as, "I'm thirsty," or as profound as, "I love you"? We do.

Who has the vision to build new and innovative services, when it becomes clear that other options in the community are woefully inadequate? We do.

And who makes it all possible? You do.

Like all things rare and precious, specialty care for children at the margins of modern medicine is expensive. And because nearly half of our patients rely on Medicaid — a program that falls far short of reimbursing costs — we face a financial gap that only generous friends like you can fill.

It should come as no surprise that, without you, Zawadi might never have donned her first pair of shoes. Without you, Grace might never have told her mom that her favorite color is red. And without you, kids might never have had on-site imaging tests without pain and fear.

The truth is that you're among an exceptional group of people committed to ensuring that all children receive the best that medicine and technology can provide — regardless of the complexity of their disabilities or the financial resources at their command.

We do a lot of special things at Gillette. Perhaps the most important, though, is to say, "Thank you" to people like you, who make it all possible.

Thank you.

2

Why We Give
Our Children Inspired Us!

The Duvalls and the Kennedys knew what Gillette's Advanced Imaging Center would mean to children who have disabilities. In fact, their own children inspired them to help make the new center a reality.

We Wanted Douglas to Feel Safe

"I want people to know that their gifts matter to children like my son."

Douglas Duvall, 9, used to cry at the mere sight of a radiology suite. Douglas requires a special tube to deliver medicines and nutrition into his small intestine. Before having surgery to place the tube permanently, Douglas frequently endured invasive X-ray procedures. At the time, Gillette didn't have advanced imaging services. "At other facilities, every visit was traumatizing," says Douglas' mom, Heather Duvall. "But without his medicines, Douglas would have seizures."

When Duvall learned that Gillette planned to build an Advanced Imaging Center, she immediately made a donation. Upon touring the new center, she learned about Gillette's positive-distraction technology, which comforts children with music, lighting and video images. "Douglas never cried during our visit!" she says. "I want people to know that their gifts matter to children like my son."

We Honored Our Daughter, Katie

Within hours of her birth in 1995, Katie Kennedy was diagnosed with microcephaly. A stroke before birth caused the condition, which results in significant neurological impairments. Given Katie's medical challenges and limited life expectancy, parents

"An on-site center is an amazing gift."

Kevin and Cindy Kennedy created The Sunshine Foundation to serve as her legacy. "The song, *You Are My Sunshine*, made Katie smile even during the most difficult hospitalizations," says Cindy Kennedy.

Katie died in February 2006, surrounded by her family. The Sunshine Foundation recently gave $17,000 to support Gillette's Advanced Imaging Center. "Traveling to off-site centers can be difficult for children and taxing for caretakers," Kennedy says. "An on-site center is an amazing gift. We hope our donation inspires others to give."

Tell Us Your Story!

What inspires you to support children who have disabilities? Please e-mail us at foundation@gillettechildrens.com. We might share your story in *Connections*.

We Need Your Help Today!

Thanks to friends like you, our Advanced Imaging Center is meeting a vital need. But we still need to raise more than $3 million for the new center. To ensure that kids continue to have on-site imaging tests without fear, we invite you to make a gift today.

You Helped Give Grace a Voice!

Mom Hears "I Love You!" for the First Time

Imagine going through childhood unable to ask questions, whisper secrets — even tell people your name. Until this spring, life without words was Grace Wright's reality. The lively 4-year-old was born with cerebral palsy, a form of brain damage that affects her ability to speak.

"We relied on rudimentary sign language and pictures to communicate," says Grace's mom, Linda Wright. "Conversations were a guessing game."

Grace's Voice — and Personality — Emerge

Grace understands language, but she couldn't express herself before coming to Gillette. Here, she tried using an augmentative and alternative communication (AAC) device. It shows pictures that represent words and phrases. When Grace touches the screen, the device "speaks" the corresponding word for her. "I learned that Grace's favorite color is red and she loves pancakes!" exclaims Wright.

Grace Inspires Mom During Cancer Battle

Shortly after Grace received her device, her mom was diagnosed with cancer and her dad lost his job to staffing cuts. Although Grace qualifies for Medicaid, her family faces limited insurance options. Wright, who also cares for two other sons with special needs, is undergoing chemotherapy. Amidst these challenges, Wright's bright light is Grace's new voice. "I never thought I'd hear my daughter say, 'I love you,'" she says. "My dream came true."

Help Us Help Families in Need

Your gifts to Gillette support state-of-the-art technology so children, like Grace, can express themselves. They also help us bring Gillette services within easy reach of struggling families. Most of all, they make life fuller — and a little brighter — for the Wrights and families just like them.

Grace says "hello" using her new device. Children's Miracle Network sponsors help Gillette purchase communication devices for patients to test at home. Each device costs at least $8,000.

Brighten a Child's Holiday

Our Wish List

- ○ Rattles
- ○ Teethers
- ○ PlayDoh toys
- ○ Coloring books
- ○ Crayons
- ○ Stickers
- ○ Matchbox cars
- ○ Etch-a-Sketch toys
- ○ Nail polish
- ○ CDs and DVDs
- ○ Nintendo Wii
- ○ Board games

For children who are hospitalized over the holidays, small gifts can bring immense joy and a sense of normalcy.

Sarah Speer still remembers how such generosity touched her life, when her brother's battle with muscular dystrophy forced her family to spend Christmas at Gillette.

"You'd think it would have been an awful Christmas," she recalls, "but the volunteers, donors and staff made it so special for the kids. There were toys, visitors and activities. It's still my favorite Christmas memory."

Speer — who works as a marketing specialist at Mid-Minnesota Federal Credit Union — now supports Gillette by raising money through Credit Unions for Kids. "My brother's experience at Gillette inspired me to give back," she says.

If you'd like to donate items from our wish list, e-mail foundation@gillettechildrens.com or call Andrew Olsen at 651-229-1766. Your generosity will brighten a child's day!

3

Make the Connection!
Make a Difference

When you support Gillette, you provide world-class medical care for children who have disabilities. And showing your support has never been easier!

What You Can Do Today

- Sign up for our e-newsletter at www.gillettechildrens.org/newsletter.
- Donate today at www.gillettechildrens.org/donate.
- Become a Guardian Angel monthly supporter by visiting www.gillettechildrens.org/guardianangels.
- Ask your employer to match gifts you make to Gillette. To see if your employer already matches gifts, visit www.matchinggifts.com/gillettechildrens.
- Recycle electronics at gillette.myboneyard.com, and the value of your used electronics will be donated to Gillette.

Just in Time for the Holidays!

Supporting Gillette is as easy as shopping for holiday gifts!

- Find the perfect gift at www.giftback.com/gillette, and 10 percent of every purchase is donated to Gillette.
- Better yet, make your purchases with a Gillette credit card. Sign up at www.gillettechildrens.org/creditcard. Gillette receives $50 the first time you use your card and 0.3 percent of every purchase made — all at no additional cost to you!

Connections is a quarterly publication of Gillette Children's Specialty Healthcare. Direct comments and questions to Andrew Olsen at 651-229-1766 or foundation@gillettechildrens.com.

4

Thank You Wal-Mart!

Zawadi Loves Her New Shoes

Wal-Mart in Maple Grove — a Children's Miracle Network sponsor — couldn't let Zawadi return to Tanzania without some new shoes. When store co-manager Mike Peckis presented a pair with pink sparkles, Zawadi's eyes lit up. "Yes!" she exclaimed. Peckis (pictured here with Zawadi and shoe department manager Joann Hogan) was just as enthusiastic. "I have goose bumps," he says. "The spirit of the kids we help is phenomenal."

Zawadi continued from Page 1

attached steel rings with struts, called fixators, to the bones in her feet and legs. Zawadi's mother then tightened the struts several times a day, slowly reshaping Zawadi's feet.

After two months of sometimes painful daily adjustments, Zawadi's feet were straight. "I never dreamed she could walk like every other child," says Zawadi's mother. "My daughter has a future!"

You Reach the World — and Your Neighborhood

Zawadi returned to Tanzania in September — with a new lease on life that you made possible. By supporting Gillette, you're providing world-class medical treatment to children for whom Gillette might be the only option. So when Zawadi says, "Thank you," we couldn't agree more.

Thanks for a Great Day!

You Helped Families Facing Disabilities Forge New Connections

Thanks to these generous sponsors, Gillette children and families recently enjoyed a day at Como Zoo filled with food, fun, prizes and — best of all — new connections!

- Checkers
- Chipotle Mexican Grill
- Costco
- Dairy Queen
- Great Clips
- IHOP
- Marriott City Center
- Marriott Depot
- Miss Minnesota

- Muller Family Theatres
- Panda Express
- Speedway/SuperAmerica
- State Farm Agent Heather Brooks Stafani
- State Farm Agent Yvonne Peterson
- Strategic Fundraising, Inc.
- Tamarack Habilitation Technologies

- Trader Joe's
- TurnKey Direct Marketing
- Wal-Mart
- Wells Fargo Private Client Group

A Special Thanks to
Momtalk.com

Meagher & Geer

CHAPTER 9

Which Are You Doing: Corporate Communications or Donor Communications?

The old newsletter Gillette sent to its donors was what many high-achieving organizations typically send: a promo piece.

The old newsletter talked about the extraordinary medicine at the hospital. It talked about the superb quality of the staff. It gave all sorts of well-deserved credit to doctors, nurses, therapists . . . and their uniquely successful treatments. And it never mentioned donors.

It was all about "us" (the insiders).

And not at all about "them" (the readers).

Look, donors don't have to read your newsletter. It's a voluntary act. Most people, in plain truth, toss it in the trash unread, immediately. (Guilty as charged.) Therefore, any particular issue of your newsletter has to be *uncommonly* interesting to hook me into a second look.

And what interests me most? Me. *Me! ME!!!*

This is a granite given: your donors are far more interested in themselves than they are in your organization.

That's not a problem, by the way. That's a huge opportunity.

Corporate communications: Not for donors

There's a technical term for the sort of newsletter Gillette used to send.

In the business communications trade, where I earned my accreditation, such newsletters—the "all about us" newsletters—classify as "corporate communications." Corporate communications are a public relations activity.

Be they newsletters, direct mail, emails, annual reports, speeches, press releases, or websites, corporate communications all have one thing in common: they are intensely focused on telling the reader how GREAT the organization is.

They also all share a favorite personal pronoun, which is "we." As in, "We did this great thing. We did that great thing." Corporate communications all push the same, simple core message: *we are very, very good at what we do*. (Some people mistakenly call this "branding." It's actually just "attempted branding," because it often fails to impress.)

Again: the chief goal of corporate communications is to build an organization's image and reputation. And with the right audience (say, stock investors, if you're a public company; or potential patients, if you're a hospital), that's exactly the right approach. But, as Gillette proved, donors are *not* the right audience. With donors, this approach yields relatively meager results.

Gillette's indisputable proof? Their newsletter took a different approach (despite fears of failure, despite doubts and internal resistance) and increased giving by 1,000 percent (again, not a misprint). That simple shift in focus—from "we are great" to "donor, you are great"—was the difference between $5,000 and $50,000 in gifts per issue.

It's your choice. But it might be a remarkably easy choice, when you consider that . . . .

Gillette Children's
FOUNDATION

Fall 2007
Volume 17, Number 3

MOMENTUM

A Newsletter for Patients, Families and Friends of Gillette Children's Specialty Healthcare

Kristin and Joey Betlej have scoliosis. Kristin, who had surgery, plays basketball and golf. She also volunteers to talk with patients undergoing similar surgery. Doctors are treating Joey with a brace. He's an avid golfer who works as a caddy in the summertime.

The John E. Lonstein Spine Care Fund was created in honor of Lonstein by his wife and children. Lonstein is an orthopaedic surgeon at Gillette. Family, friends, colleagues and patients provided additional funding. The fund supports projects and programs benefiting Gillette patients who have spinal disorders. Projects include picture books for preschoolers and printed, video and Web information for teenagers. For information about the fund, contact Scott Nelson at 651-229-1720 or snelson@gillettechildrens.com.

INSIDE

At Gillette, Medical Pioneers Set the Standards for Spine Care

Since 1947, doctors and specialists at Gillette Children's Specialty Healthcare have established principles that are still considered the highest standards of care for children with spine deformities. Kristin and Joey Betlej are two in a long line of patients who have benefited from the hard work and dedication of Gillette's medical pioneers.

Kristin Betlej is an elegant, statuesque 17-year-old with a warm smile. As a high-school junior, she plays basketball and golf. In addition she takes jazz, ballet and tap dance lessons and plays baritone in the school band. Her brother, Joey Betlej, 13, is a well-spoken young man whose confident demeanor belies his young age. He plays basketball, tennis and golf and is a trombonist.

Both Kristin and Joey have scoliosis, a sideways curvature of the spine that can shape it into a single curve (like the letter C) or into two curves (like the letter S). About 3 percent of children have some type of scoliosis. One in every 200 of those children requires treatment. Doctors customize treatments to each child's particular needs.

Tailoring Treatments

When Kristin was in third grade, her pediatrician grew concerned about the curve of her spine, especially in light of her family history of scoliosis. "Kristin's grandmother didn't have treatment," explains Kit Betlej, Kristin's mother. "She has a noticeable curve, is unable to lift things and can't walk for any distance."

"Kristin's doctor said her curve looked different from the typical scoliosis curve," Betlej adds. "Typically, the spine curves to the right. Kristin's went to the left and didn't have the S curve." She had pain when she knelt and couldn't sit comfortably for any length of time.

As a result, Kristin began wearing a brace when she was 8. Because of the unusual curve, her family discussed the possibility of spine-fusion surgery with John Lonstein, M.D., an orthopaedic surgeon at Gillette. Spine fusion surgery involves joining several spine bones to make one unit. The procedure is used to partially correct the curve and to stop curves from progressing. During surgery, surgeons implant a smooth rod attached to the spine by hooks, screws and wires to hold the spine in place while fusion occurs.

Doctors also kept an eye on Joey. At 9, he had an X-ray indicating that he, too, has scoliosis. For the past 18 months, he's been wearing a brace for 23 hours a day. The brace is lightweight and worn under clothing. He'll wear it until he's done growing. "The brace really doesn't prevent me from doing anything," he says. "I can take it off when I play basketball, tennis or golf."

The Betlejs' experience is markedly different from that of past patients.

The Story Unfolds

In the early years, at Gillette and elsewhere, doctors treated scoliosis with exercises or casts, which often failed to keep the curve of the spine from progressing. In 1947, John Moe, M.D., established the Spine Service at Gillette. He brought together a team — including brace makers, nurses, surgery staff and physicians — to work with children who had spine deformities. Working with the team of specialists, Moe used advanced braces for treating scoliosis and developed practical surgical techniques that resulted in a good fusion.

By the time he retired, Moe was known as the father of modern scoliosis surgery.

A Breakthrough Idea

Throughout the 1950s, doctors treated spine deformities, such as Kristin's, with a Milwaukee brace to support the entire spine and to keep a spinal curve from progressing. The brace extended to the neck and wasn't easily hidden under clothing. Surgeons also did fusion surgery, using bone grafts without screws and rods to stop the progression of the curve. Following surgery, patients spent one year in casts. Often the bones didn't knit properly, and patients had second surgeries, which meant another year of casts.

In 1959, Robert Winter, M.D., was an orthopaedic resident at the University of Minnesota. He completed two rotations in pediatric orthopaedics at Gillette. "During my first rotation, significant things happened," he says.

A Texas surgeon, Paul Harrington, M.D., had developed a system of stainless steel rods and hooks that he surgically implanted in scoliosis patients to straighten and hold the realigned curvature of the spine. Moe, a skilled surgeon, understood the value of the rods for spine fusions, and he invited Harrington to demonstrate the technique at Gillette. Winter assisted with the surgeries. We became one of the first hospitals in the country to use Harrington rods.

"With internal rods, and a good cast, children healed better, and we could get them up walking within two weeks," Winter explains. When Winter completed his residency, Moe invited him to join the Gillette Spine Service. Throughout their tenure, these and other Gillette physicians and staff assembled surgical techniques and bracing technology to revolutionize spine care.

*Spine Care —
continued on Page 6*

This front-cover helped raise $4,470 in gifts from a pool of 20,000 recipients. Notice the headline: it puts the hospital front and center. The 1,200-word article is an in-depth essay concerning the evolution of a sophisticated treatment for spine curvature. *(Reprinted with Permission)*

Gillette Children's
Specialty Healthcare

A CHILDREN'S MIRACLE
NETWORK AFFILIATE

Bringing You Closer to
the Lives You Help Change

Connections

Fall 2008 • Volume 1 • Number 1

Zawadi Says, "Thank You!"

You Helped a Tanzanian Girl Stand Tall on Her Own Two Feet

To meet Zawadi Rajabu, 6, is to experience gratitude through the eyes of a child. She greets you with a warm hug, a bright smile, and an emphatic, "Thank you!" Before you can grasp why you deserve such adoration, you catch a mischievous glint in her eye. "No catch me!" she taunts, running in the opposite direction. Another game of tag has begun, and — just like that — *you're it*.

It's an idyllic scene, but Zawadi's story doesn't begin here. Before she could even dream of chasing about in sparkly sneakers, Zawadi needed feet on which to stand.

Her Community Believed She Was Cursed

Zawadi was born with two clubfeet in an impoverished village outside Arusha, Tanzania. Her community saw the disability as a curse, and local children threw stones at her.

Zawadi's father abandoned the family the day she was born, leaving her mother to care for three children alone. "Zawadi would have no future if something happened to me," says Zawadi's mother, Sofia, through an interpreter.

Few Could Help Her

Zawadi's fate changed when missionaries Tom and Polly Wiley spotted her. "She had huge brown eyes and a penetrating look," Tom Wiley recalls. "We knew we had to help her."

The Wileys discovered that Zawadi's case was too severe for treatment in Tanzania. She

needed a surgeon trained in the Ilizarov method — a complex technique for reshaping bones, developed by Gavriil Ilizarov, M.D., in a remote Siberian hospital. It was a tall order, to be sure.

But a Google search quickly uncovered one of the few surgeons in the world who could help Zawadi: Mark Dahl, M.D., pediatric orthopaedic surgeon at Gillette Children's Specialty Healthcare. In fact, Dahl trained in Siberia with Ilizarov himself.

"My Daughter Has a Future!"

Within weeks, Zawadi flew to St. Paul for a treatment that Dahl had performed thousands of times, but on only a few children with Zawadi's condition. During a five-hour surgery, Dahl

Zawadi continued on Page 4

Because of You!

Zawadi wears sparkly new shoes
Page 1

Douglas can visit an imaging center without crying
Page 2

Katie's memory continues to inspire
Page 2

Grace can say, "I love you!"
Page 3

Without treatment in Tanzania, Zawadi (right) learned to walk on the rough calluses that formed where her feet should be.

But today, Zawadi (above) is shopping for her first pairs of shoes! Wal-Mart helped her find shoes that fit around her braces, which will keep her feet straight while she grows.

This front-cover helped raise $49,600 in gifts from the same 20,000 recipients. The headline gives the credit to (and liberally thanks) the donor. This 500-word article tells the inspiring tale of an African child, born deformed, who journeyed to Gillette and got her feet turned in the right direction. *(Reprinted with Permission)*

I've saved the best part for last: when you *stop* doing corporate communications and instead embrace *true* donor communications, the labor of creating your newsletter is likely to shrink and become more manageable.

A good donor newsletter will be blessedly brief, its articles blessedly short, its tone more conversational than academic. It will not be pure reporting. It will read more like a chatty phone call to your best friend. How hard is that?

PART II

How Newsletters Fit In

CHAPTER 10

Extraordinary Experiences

S imone Joyaux, ACFRE, author of *Strategic Fund Development* *(3rd edition)*, calls them "extraordinary experiences." It's a phrase she borrowed for the fundraising profession from some other deep thinker whose special study is customer satisfaction.

They are those unusual, eye-opening, "ah-ha!" personal experiences that draw the donor deeper into the organization.

They can be anything.

Sometimes they're just *a few moments long*. A board member surprises a new donor with a phone call saying "thank you" for that first gift. Maybe a little conversation ensues.

Sometimes, though, they are *unforgettable* "sense memories."

Sense memories are those that linger because you have personally touched, heard, seen, smelled, or tasted something remarkable. Sense memories can (science says) last a lifetime.

- A zoo offers its donors a well-supervised chance to feed wild animals.

- A fundraiser for a charity that aids immigrants brings her donors along to the airport to greet new refugees. If there's a child arriving, the donor gets a teddy bear to offer as a welcome.

- A hospital conducting research on Alzheimer's invites donors to watch a surgeon probe the brain of a cadaver, looking for clues.

- A museum director leads the way into climate-controlled vaults where restoration work is done . . . and hands the donor a perfectly balanced 2,000-year-old sword that feels alive . . . and murderous.

- Supporters of a women's fund attending the annual gala watch a deeply moving little documentary of a single mom's painful but successful struggle to reinvent herself. The room goes black. A spotlight strikes the podium—and there's the star of the documentary herself, offering donors her personal thanks. Tears flow. Checkbooks open.

All true instances, incidentally.

Donor newsletters: Extraordinary experiences . . . for the rest of us

The only problem with extraordinary experiences is this: they reach so few people.

Audience penetration is likely to be by the onesies and twosies. For every donor that *does* enjoy an extraordinary experience with your organization, there are probably dozens, maybe thousands, who never get the chance.

To the rescue: the humble *charity newsletter*.

Your newsletter is the single best way I know to deliver extraordinary experiences into every donor's home on a regular basis.

Consider again Adrian Sargeant's research into donor loyalty. One of his seven essentials for retaining donors is this: "Donors are learning. You're taking them on a journey."

Fundraisers used to talk about "educating the donor." By which they meant turning outsiders into insiders.

If you banged on long enough, the theory went—pounding statistics into donors' thick skulls—then eventually they'd see the problem the way staff saw the problem and begin forking over more money. It made sense, in a cartoon Neanderthal sort of way: you get the girl, not by wooing her . . . but by knocking her unconscious with your intellectual club.

It didn't have a prayer of working, of course; as any respectable psychologist will attest. Educators, here is what your donor wished to scream in your face: "I don't want to go to your *school*. If you think passing a test on a charity is some kind of pleasure, think again. I will bloody well 'educate' myself, thank you. And, by the way, your statistics are a big, smelly bore."

Today, we call the "getting to know you" process by a kinder, gentler name: "cultivation." Of course, the ultimate goal is still the same, despite the name change: "More money, please."

But the change isn't just cosmetic. True cultivation really *is* different. Much nicer. Less imperious. Organizations deliver fewer lectures. They put away the charts and graphs. They tell more stories.

They focus on delivering *emotional gratification* to their donors (at least, the most successful do).

Savvy organizations flatter the donor. Savvy organizations tell their donors how important they are. And—key point—savvy organizations are totally sincere in their flattery. Because donors *are* desperately important in the nonprofit world. They are your investors. They are your fuel.

And their continued loyalty is the real reason for your newsletter.

SPANA is an animal welfare charity based in the UK. This centerfold from its donor newsletter fully satisfies one of Adrian Sargeant's seven dicta for improving loyalty: "Take your donors on a journey." Actually, there are three journeys on this page. Journey #1: the sequential photography documenting the animal's misery. Journey #2: the map showing where the donors' contributions have gone to work. And journey #3: the opportunity to help ("What you can do today"). *(Reprinted with Permission)*

CHAPTER 11

Following in the Footsteps of Your Message

Even amazingly effective charities can get things wrong on occasion. Here's a mistake I ran across while doing an audit. Call it "The Case of the Message That Disappeared." It goes something like this . . . .

- To *acquire* new donors, this organization sent out direct mail appeals that boldly, on the outbound envelope, challenged Christians to "follow where your faith would lead you" and help the poor.

- And yet . . . the newsletter that reported back to these donors didn't echo this faith-based message. Instead, the nonprofit's newsletter talked about the work in the field the same way a secular organization might, using a straight-ahead reporting style brimming with statistics but devoid of spiritual content.

- Result? The newsletter landed few additional contributions from individuals.

They bought you for a reason

Donors give to your organization for their own good reasons. And those reasons are often firmly attached to a set of personal core values; for instance, feeling a religious duty to help the poor.

New donors who've responded to a message such as "follow in the footsteps of your faith" will likely respond to the same kind of message again. And again. And again. Don't save those messages just for appeals. Litter those same messages across *all* your donor communications including newsletters.

Some of your donors, maybe most of them, are "values donors." They follow in the footsteps of their faith in *all* their philanthropy:

when they give to the arts, when they give to education, when they give to social justice. Core values run deep and seldom change. Adrian Sargeant discovered that donor loyalty depended on just seven things. One of that handful: "Your donors share your beliefs."

By the way, organizational silos were the true villains in "The Case of the Message That Disappeared." It's a big charity. The direct mail group is on one floor, working for the fundraising department. The newsletter people are on another floor, working for the communications department. And never the twain happened to meet.

Newsletter editors: have samples of your organization's successful direct mail in front of you as you write. Look for key sales messages like "follow in the footsteps of your faith." Use the same kinds of messages in your newsletter headlines. Reaffirm the values that first brought your donors aboard.

They chose your charity for a reason, when they gave that first time. Your donor newsletter should reflect, not neglect, that reason.

Anatomy of a failed front page

The Joe DiMaggio Children's Hospital is among America's best. It is eminently worthy of support. Yet the donor newsletter produced almost no revenue. "People tell us they like the newsletter," the foundation office reported. "But nobody ever sends a check. What do you think is wrong?"

I saw four errors.

- **Error #1: The headline sends exactly the wrong message.** There is one thing I can guarantee: almost everyone encountering this front page will read the headline first. How do I know? Because I'm familiar with eye-motion studies. Those studies show that my eye (and yours) goes immediately—involuntarily, actually—to the biggest or most pronounced graphics on a printed page. It's just how the brain works. And what is the most pronounced graphic here? The headline. And what message does this headline convey loud and clear. This headline says, in effect: "We just brought in a ton of money." From which the donor can safely conclude, "Well, you don't need me! At least not now . . . ."

- **Error #2: No children who need our help.** There are 30 people depicted on this front page; 29 are festive adults in evening wear.

- **Error #3: The magic word "you" is absent.** The easiest way to stop hurrying readers is to use the word "you"—in your headline, if at all possible. This front page never once mentions "you," so it's impersonal rather than personal.

- **Error #4: The front-page story has nothing to do with the mission.** What is the subliminal message emanating from this front page? "A good time was had by all." The party was fun. Attendees went home with smiles on their faces. Is devoting a newsletter's front page, its most important real estate, to a fabulous party a bad idea? Absolutely. You're elevating second-rank information to a first-ranked position. The hospital's philanthropic mission has nothing to do with parties, it has to do with healing gravely sick kids. Stay focused.

Memorial Foundation ◆ Joe DiMaggio Children's Hospital Foundation

CHRONICLE

WINTER 2010

AN INVITATION TO INVEST IN YOUR HEALTHCARE

Fairy Tale Ball Raises $270,000 for Children and Families at Joe DiMaggio Children's Hospital

It was an unforgettable action-packed, two-day event filled with entertainment, golf, a gala and poignant moments of reflection as more than 550 guests danced the night away to classic rock's biggest names, including Clarence Clemons, Steve Augeri (formerly of Journey), and Wally Palmer from The Romantics. **The 7th Annual Fairy Tale Ball "Mulan,"** presented by the Diamond Angels of Joe DiMaggio Children's Hospital Foundation was hosted and sponsored in part by The Westin Diplomat Resort and Spa.

Guests enjoyed the festivities which ultimately help the littlest members of our community. The impact of the Fairy Tale Ball was brought clearly into focus as attendees heard the story of this year's ambassador, Maggie, a healthy eighteen-month-old who weighed only 11 ounces at birth.

The majority of funds raised will support the new recently expanded Wasie NICU at Joe DiMaggio Children's Hospital, a state-of-the-art 64-bed facility that cares for South Florida's most acutely ailing newborn babies made possible by The Wasie Foundation. Over $19,000 of the evening's proceeds will support the Diamond Angels Family Fund, which provides families of children with life-threatening conditions being treated at the hospital, with emergency financial support for non-medical

expenses. During its seven years, the Fairy Tale Ball has raised nearly $2 million.

"When we conceptualized this event, we chose to call it the Fairy Tale Ball and use a different fairy tale as the theme for each year," said Babette Ferre-Kosar, who along with Wendy Palmer, co-chaired this year's tales show central characters faced with over-whelming obstacles, but they all triumphed in the end."

Drs. Allan and Ronnie Greissman with Maxine and Dr. Robert Davis

Maggie is the smallest baby ever born and cared for at Joe DiMaggio Children's Hospital's Wasie Neonatal Intensive Care Unit (NICU) and is a living example of hope and survival. Born prematurely, Maggie underwent 35 blood transfusions and three surgeries and after five months was discharged from the hospital. She continues to meet milestones, amaze her parents and has not

This year's Diamond Angels ambassador, Maggie with two of her NICU doctors and her parents. Pictured (L-R): Dr. Bruce Schulman, Maggie's parents, Maggie and Dr. Lester McIntyre.

needed to be readmitted to the hospital, thanks to the extraordinary medical care she received early in her life.

At birth Maggie's tiny body was fragile, but her will to live was strong. Thanks to the Diamond Angels and other donors, the Wasie NICU saved Maggie's life. Every day the NICU is full of babies like Maggie, struggling to survive. For more information on how you can help the tiniest of our patients, please contact the Foundation office at 954-265-3454.

Larry Reiss, event co-chair Wendy Palmer, Hon. Nicholas Lopane, and Drs. Marietta and Ira Glazer

Howard Friedman, event co-chair Babette Ferre-Kosar, Bonnie Fenster, and Diamond Angels President Sharon Truske with her husband, Tom

Sherrie Kukulski with her husband Mark, General Manager of the Diplomat Resort and Spa

Tara and James Disbinger

Jorge Flores, Janet Flores, Frank Sacco, Rebecca Caschette, and Sylvia and Al Gil

Dr. Jason Adler, Mandee Heller Adler and Drs. Nick and Wendy Masi

The Joe DiMaggio Children's Hospital is among America's best. It is eminently worthy of support. Yet the donor newsletter produced almost no revenue. "People tell us they like the newsletter," the foundation office reported. "But nobody ever sends a check. What do you think is wrong?" *(Reprinted with Permission)*

CHAPTER 12

The Research and the Reality

In 1995, The Russ Reid Company in conjunction with George Barna of the Barna Research Group, conducted a landmark study of U.S. donors.

Reid/Barna's "Heart of the Donor" study quizzed a random sample of 1,164 donors across America about their preferences and opinions.

Among its questions, the study asked donors how the nonprofits they supported could best "keep in touch [and] help you feel more closely connected to and interested in the work of the organization."

The study said, "We identified a single stand-out: newsletters. Almost three-quarters of all donors claimed that receiving a regular newsletter would increase their focus upon and interest in an organization."

At the time of the study, Amazon was just a year old. No one really knew if the idea of an online bookseller would work. The Internet itself was still a novelty, not yet integrated into everyday life. The donors Reid/Barna interviewed had been born in the Roaring Twenties and Great Depression.

So that was then. Is 1995 research still relevant?

Absolutely, in my view.

First, these were seriously good researchers; the results were solid.

Second? Look: a newsletter is a reporting mechanism.

Do you still need to tell your donors today what you did with their hard-earned money? Yes. Of course you do. That's one of your primary responsibilities, on the donor communications front.

And why is it so important, from a business sense? Because if you *don't* report to them, you will fulfill their already dim expectations of nonprofits. And hence they will probably not give again.

Sure, donors want a newsletter. They just don't read it.

So I'm in favor of donor newsletters. Yet Jerry Panas, one of America's most experienced fundraisers and author of the classic book *Asking*, insists, "Every time we survey, donors tell us they don't read the newsletters."

Contradiction? Not really.

Over the years, I've reviewed hundreds of newsletters from nonprofits of all sorts and sizes. Many of these newsletters, maybe most, shared the same handful of bad habits. In fact, let's call them what they really are: *Fatal Flaws*. Why fatal? Because these nine flaws *kill* interest.

You'll learn what they are—and how to avoid them—in Section 3 of this book.

CHAPTER 13

You Are an Intrusion

Communications from nonprofits have to survive in a brutal, breakneck, unforgiving world. Getting heard is tougher than ever. Consider:

- "We now consume about 100,000 words each day from various media, which is a whopping 350% increase over what we handled back in 1980." *Source: science journalist Winifred Gallagher, quoted in The New York Times, Feb 2012*

- "[By the new millennium] the average Westerner was . . . taking in as many images in 24 hours as a Victorian saw in a lifetime." *Source: The New York Times, December 2010*

- In 1990, the Internet didn't exist as a consumer channel. By 2010, the American adult was spending 13 hours per week on the Internet—*recreationally*, in addition to working there. Every year that "Internet percentage" soars. The pool of "disposable attention span" is shrinking fast.

Every day, thousands of messages come at you from every direction (TV, radio, the Internet, your morning newspaper, magazines, billboards, the packages on your shelf, the trucks on the highway, your mail), sent by organizations trying to penetrate your brain and influence your behavior . . . particularly your spending behavior (which, of course, includes charitable giving).

Your mailbox is one of the busier bees. Direct marketers are nothing if not persistent. (This is probably a good place to note that your donor newsletter is just another piece of direct mail, from the recipient's point of view.)

In desperate self-defense of their privacy and sanity, people have the habit of sorting their mail into three stacks:

- **Stack #1:** Stuff they don't dare ignore . . . because if they do, something bad will happen. Bills go into this stack.

- **Stack #2:** Stuff they can safely ignore. Catalogs. Direct mail offers. Solicitations from unfamiliar causes. *This is the biggest stack by far.* This stack goes straight to the trash unread.

- **Stack #3:** Stuff they're somewhat interested in, intrigued by, or that shares their values. "Maybe I'd enjoy spending a little time here." Your newsletter's goal is to earn a spot in this stack.

But getting into stack #3 means, first of all, eliminating fatal flaws, the ones described in Section 3.

Second, always remember: donors automatically view your newsletter (as they view every other incoming message) as an intrusion, until proven innocent—or, more aptly, until proven *interesting*.

If your newsletter *is* interesting, though, it will become in time a welcome part of the donor's life, every issue adding another chapter to the ongoing adventure novel, *How My Gifts Saved a Piece of the World*.

CHAPTER 14

E-newsletters:
What Are They Good For?

E mailed newsletters have their uses:

- Emailed newsletters can play a minor, yet useful, supporting role in the retention of donors. I have no science. But it makes complete sense that a frequently emailed newsletter would do some good and no harm. It shows the flag. Reminds people you exist. Reinforcing the brand. Whether it's opened or not, every e-newsletter arriving in an in-box conveys a basic (but important) message: "Yes, we're still here fighting the good fight . . . ."

- Emailed newsletters are good at promoting upcoming events. (Typical subject line: "Check out our fall line-up of sizzling theatre.") I asked Kerri Karvetski, a true online guru, founder of Company K Media, to recommend her favorite emailed news-letters. She named two: *Thirteen Week*, published by NY Public Media; and *Smithsonian Focus*, a guide to new exhibits. Both promote upcoming schedules.

- They're good if you want to sell things to your base, such as tickets to events and great programs. (Subject line: "We're down to the last few seats. Order now.")

- They are good at reaching people fast, in an emergency. ("Our steeple just blew off!" "Family burned out of house and home. Will you help?")

- They're good at creating buzz and support around a white-hot issue. ("We didn't think it could get any worse. But it just did. Speak out now!")

- They are good at reminders. ("Clothing drive tomorrow. Are your donations at the curb?") One organization emails a monthly

Wish List that attracts good response. Items are personalized: "An umbrella and raincoat for Pearlie." "A collapsible grocery cart for Deborah who just moved into an apartment." "Clarence needs sturdy work pants (40 waist x 32 length)."

- They're good at "save this date" bulletins.

- They are good at linking people deeper into your material, to "read more" on a blog or website. ("Parents: Don't miss our online update on autism news.")

- They're more acceptable to younger audiences.

But.

Spoiler alert: Emailed newsletters are fundraising duds, says one expert

"I'm getting close to concluding that e-newsletters don't work," Jeff Brooks wrote me recently.

Jeff, whom I've mentioned previously, is now a senior creative director with TrueSense, a direct mail house. (He's got a terrific book to his credit, too: *The Fundraiser's Guide to Irresistible Communications*). TrueSense services heavyweight clients like The Salvation Army and Ronald McDonald House Charities.

I'd contacted him, hunting model e-newsletters I could share in this book.

"We no longer do e-newsletters for any of our clients," he replied, "because response has been so low."

Jeff's theory and his tests

Like all successful direct mail people, Jeff Brooks worships testing and data. "You have to measure what you're doing," as he says, "or you're clueless."

As its basic measure of effectiveness for e-newsletters, his firm decided "to go by open rate rather than response . . . ." It made sense. Emails are like direct mail appeals in this regard: if people don't open the email (or envelope, in direct mail), the rest of the mechanism has no chance to work.

The opening rate was lousy.

"[We] found it was extremely low and varied little." How low is low? Constant Contact tracks opening rates for emailed newsletters originating from all sorts of organizations. Their nonprofit opening rate averages around 20 percent. Jeff saw opening rates well below that.

The opening rate improved slightly when the subject line was topical, rather than something routine like *May e-news*. "But it was still low," says Jeff. With print newsletters, envelope teasers as routine as "Your Latest Donor Newsletter Inside" are adequate. Emailed newsletters need something more.

He has a working theory. Jeff thinks "the 'leaning back' psychology of print newsletters ('Let's see what's interesting here . . . ') just doesn't activate for most people when they're online, which is overwhelmingly a 'leaning forward' situation. I think fanatics may 'lean forward' for a newsletter . . . but very few donors are fanatics."

One solution he's testing: "Make every article or item you would put in your newsletter into its own email. One email, one topic. Too early to say if it's a real solution. The risk is increased *unsubscribes* because frequency is too high for some recipients."

Jeff now sends out emails with just one call to action. "Doesn't have to be 'give,' but should be something—sign a petition, write an encouraging message, click to give, take a quiz, etc."

Giving "your people" lots of highly focused chances to ACT NOW might do the trick in the click-crazy, hyper-kinetic online environment. Instant gratification is always popular. On the other hand . . . .

Jeff Brooks ended his note: "I think this shows how undeveloped e-fundraising still is. We haven't figured out how to do some of the most basic things in the medium."

On the other hand . . . .

Karen Affeld, Director of Development at the Lady Bird Johnson Wildflower Center, in June 2012 wrote to describe her successes using emailed newsletters.

"The Wildflower Center has no fewer than four different e-newsletters."

- Monthly Wildflower Wire goes to a regional/local audience.

- Monthly Wildflower Watch focuses on topics of national interest.

- Weekly What's Coming Up at the Wildflower Center is a calendar (and attendance prompt).

- And finally there's a "weekly e-wire for our gift store."

The total count: two monthly e-newsletters, two weekly e-newsletters. The metrics: the Wildflower Center has 20,000+ email subscribers; with an enviable opening rate of 25 percent. *Please note: every subject line contains the word "wildflower."* Those 10 characters do the work. They connect directly to the core interest of the prospect: "wildflower."

Karen graciously shared lots of details about her overall program. "This year, we switched to doing email-only annual appeals and so far it's been very successful. We've gotten substantial donations from people who had never given before and our net proceeds from the appeals are WAY up.

"The e-appeals go out to all subscribers to our various newsletters, where our direct mail annual appeals were sent out only to prior donors due to the high cost of printing and mailing.

"We still use direct mail for membership acquisition mailings and for renewal reminders but everything else has gone digital for us. We do mail a quarterly glossy magazine to members, but it's not a fundraising vehicle."

Can *any* charity switch to an all-digital approach . . . or does it help to be a photogenic, event-heavy charity with "fanatical" followers, like the Wildflower Center?

Here's Karen bottom line: "Why do I think our e-newsletters work for us? They're very content rich, with links to more information on our web site. They're attractive, with nice photos and graphics. And they help us build a more engaged audience that cares enough about our work to donate."

The digital experience isn't the same as the paper experience

"People *use* the web," TJ Larkin notes. "They *read* paper."

Dr. Larkin is the author, with his wife, Sandar, of a McGraw Hill business book called *Communicating Change*. Their clients include top corporations, as well as major entities like NASA.

And those two well-chosen verbs, *use* and *read*, pretty much sum up all the difference between online and paper.

When I published the first edition of this book, in 2005, the question in the air was very much:

"How soon can I abandon my paper newsletter and switch to an emailed version instead?"

It was the most commonly asked question at my workshops. And the craving for change made complete sense. Donor newsletters cost money and produced nothing tangible, fundraisers (who had not discovered the Domain formula) groused. There were heavy printing costs. There were heavy postage costs. And print newsletters required desktop publishing skills. Which were hard to find.

On the other hand (the argument went), emailed newsletters cost nothing, except somebody's time. E-newsletters could be really short, too. "Even if I can't write a lick, I can probably compose 50 words of coherent prose."

Hence, switching to emailed newsletters looked like a guaranteed "win-win." Then along came Facebook, incorporated in 2004.

In 2004, my working assumption was that emailed newsletters would play an increasingly important role in bringing in gifts, as we all burrowed into our online existence. I assumed emailed newsletters would be the "next gen" delivery system for nonprofit news.

As it turned out, however . . . .

Email did not ascend the throne, to grab an increasing share of the world's online attention span. Email was rudely shoved aside, by Facebook and a galaxy of other social networking options vying for our attention.

To paraphrase the immortal advice of Kris Hermanns, "If you're not getting good results from a printed newsletter, why would you think you'll get better results from an emailed newsletter? Switching media doesn't matter. Knowing what you're doing matters."

Younger donors respond to mobile, not paper news, Australian tests show

Age matters. In the US, most donors are older. Fully 68 percent of the donors who respond to True Sense mailings are 55 and older;

46 percent are 65 and older. Younger donors exist in large numbers, but only where so-called "street fundraising" is common, as it is in Australia.

Are younger donors as responsive as older donors to paper newsletters? Apparently not.

Jonathon Grapsas, founder of Flat Earth Direct, a digital and direct mail agency in Australia, swears: "Late 20's, early 30's: sending them stuff that our DM donors (55–75ish) would love . . . frankly bores the hell out of this group. We're sending long, paper-based comms when these guys want short, punchy, dynamic, mobile friendly touch points."

So, with younger donors, Jonathon's firm has been testing smartphone and tablet-based communications. Mobile communications are working, too: retention for young donors acquired through street fundraising (also known as face-to-face outside the US) has improved.

He reported, "The average month 1 attrition was 13 percent," for newly acquired younger donors, a notoriously skittish bunch. "We've now got this down to an average of 4 percent," thanks to the new mobile donor communications. "Three-month attrition used to average 21 percent, now down to 7 percent. And so on."

A ray of hope: What might make emailed newsletters special

Mark Phillips, founder and CEO of UK's profoundly gifted Bluefrog agency, listed in June 2012 three "barriers to giving" he's observed:

- **The risk is too great.** Donors don't trust you that much. You need to give donors things to do that only cost modest (i.e., less risky) sums.

- **It's too much hassle.** "I don't want to find a pen and write a check." Even digging out a credit card is painful, so you have to work extra hard to ease them past this obstacle. (Note to self: *always* talk in fundraising materials about how **easy** it is to make a difference **now**.)

- **Boredom.** Mark advises, "If you can give people something new and interesting to do, they'll often do it."

Online newsletters should be ideal for surmounting all of those obstacles. *Assuming* your subscribers react positively to the 40 or less characters in your subject line and therefore open the email.

Which, again, mostly they don't and won't. But that's just the brutal reality of our busy online lives.

Final word to Kerri Karvetski, Company K Media

"Email newsletters aren't going to be your biggest fundraisers," Kerri admits, "but that doesn't mean you shouldn't fundraise in email newsletters. I would:

- Put a soft ask at the bottom (P.S., footer)

- Occasionally include opportunities to give such as honor and memorial gifts, especially for holidays; symbolic gifts such as adoptions and shares (think Heifer); and store items such as t-shirts, mugs, etc.

"You're just going to have to adjust your expectations down.

"Best format for an emailed newsletter? Essentially, a few well-chosen items (much less than print), with jumps to larger stories. Try to include opportunities for engagement such as quizzes, asking for comments on blog posts, share to Facebook and Twitter, share-your-story-type activities.

"And with the trend toward more and more people reading email on mobile devices, these newsletters are evolving—bigger fonts, big buttons instead of links (easier for fingertips to follow), streamlined layout (one column vs. two).

"Fundraising following advocacy (petition and pledge signing), even as close as on the advocacy confirmation action page, is a good tactic, too."

GrowSmartRI
Sustainable Economic Growth & Quality of Place

2013 Smart Growth LegWrap

Innovative News & Tools for People Shaping our Communities

July, 2013

2013 LegWrap

**Grow Smart Rhode Island
Board of Directors**

Dear Tom

You're among the **4,479** civic leaders, state & local officials, development professionals, investors, decision-makers and visionary citizens getting the latest news, happenings and trends in the local smart growth movement.

We're Grow Smart Rhode Island. Partner with us. Support us with a tax deductible contribution. Let's make Rhode Island a better place together by playing to our strengths.

Historic Tax Credit back to work for RI; advances for agricultural vitality; Transit funding reform left at the altar... again

What I like about this "legislative wrap-up" from GrowSmartRI is the personalized introduction. "Dear Tom, You're among the 4,479 civic leaders…." author John Flaherty reminds me. In other words, it's a small group of real people who care about sustainable growth. Also, I love hearing that I'm a "leader." Even though, in fact, I'm not any kind of leader on this issue, my brain accepts every compliment gratefully. That's just the way human brains are: they crave flattery. *(Reprinted with Permission)*

CHAPTER 15

Email Subject Lines

Like direct mail envelopes, email subject lines have just one purpose: to get opened. When they're opened, the rest of the mechanism has a chance to work. If they're not opened? Dead air. Nothing happens.

During the 2012 U.S. Presidential campaign, Barack Obama's team raised $690 million online, mostly through emails. "The campaign would test multiple drafts and subject lines—often as many as 18 variations—before picking a winner to blast out to tens of millions of subscribers," reported Bloomberg Businessweek in a post-contest analysis. In the process, the team learned some interesting things.

"The subject lines that worked best were things you might see in your in-box from other people," said Toby Fallsgraff, the campaign's email director. "'Hey' was probably the best one we had over the duration." Also a big winner for Obama among his base: "I will be outspent."

Another surprise to the team: ugly sells. That's a long-recognized phenomenon in physical direct mail, of course; but now we know it works in emails, too. And what does "ugly" mean? It is the opposite of smart, sleek, hip, pretty, and polished to perfection.

Amelia Showalter, the Obama campaign's director of digital analytics, confessed, "We were so bad at predicting what would win. Every time something really ugly won, it would shock me: giant-size fonts for links, plain-text links vs. pretty 'Donate' buttons. Eventually we got to thinking, 'How could we make things even less attractive?' That's how we arrived at the ugly yellow highlighting on the sections we wanted to draw people's eye to."

You don't have to campaign for the White House, though, to have profitable fun with email subject lines.

I'm a fan of the subject lines written by Achieve Hartford!, an urban school reform group in Connecticut. Its monthly e-newsletter is vitally important, because it's the main way the group talks to its base.

Achieve Hartford! intrigues it subscribers with enticing, but not fully revealed subject lines like these (everyone in the office contributes ideas, and they don't steer away from controversy):

- Not . . . Often . . . Enough
- Believing in Success
- A Rhythm of Ownership
- In the Red
- Signed, Sealed and Delivered
- Reform: Dead End or Detour?
- The Iron is Hot

PART III

Techniques

CHAPTER 16

These Nine "Fatal Flaws" Kill Response

Almost every donor newsletter I see suffers from at least one of the following fatal flaws, listed in no particular order.

Notice: I didn't say "moderately destructive" flaws nor "mildly offensive" flaws. These nine flaws are grave. You'd be shocked by how many donor newsletters suffer from all nine.

Flaw #1: Your newsletter avoids using the word "you." A good donor newsletter is friendly, even intimate, in tone. It embraces the reader in a very obvious way by generously using the word "you," especially in the headlines. If you insist instead on a corporate voice (a lot of "we did this, we did that"), you'll keep your readers at arm's length and prevent them from crawling into your lap for a head rub (cat lovers will know what I'm talking about).

Flaw #2: Your newsletter has no emotional triggers. It's cold (data driven), not hot (story driven). Restrained, not flattering. Corporate, not loving. No anger. No hope. No joy. Wrong: tugging the heart-strings is a full-time job, if you're serious about raising money.

Flaw #3: You claim it's a newsletter (i.e., a bearer of news). But it's not: it's really just an excuse to say, "Hi! We'd like to sell you stuff."

Flaw #4: Your front page is boring. I hope this phenomenon is fading. But last time I did a major survey of charity newsletters, I was shocked to see that the majority devoted their front pages to a recurring, less-than-inspiring letter "from the desk of" the executive director or board chair, usually without a real headline. ("From the desk of . . . ." is not a headline; it's just a column label.) Don't fall for this bad convention. Your front page is where first impressions are formed. Reserve it for important news.

Flaw #5: No "accomplishment reporting." This is a key item in the Domain Formula. Your newsletter is supposed to answer the basic questions: "What did you do with my gift? How did philanthropy help?"

Flaw #6: Your newsletter isn't "donor-centered." The job of donor communications, in my view, is to make the donor feel needed and wanted. A good newsletter will tell donors they're making an important difference in the world, they *are* good people . . . over and over and over. Their interest in your organization will quickly wane if you fail to deliver on this.

Flaw #7: Your newsletter depends far too much on statistics (and far too little on anecdotes) to make your case for support.

Researching charitable impulses, Duke psychology professor, Dan Ariely, uncovered in his exacting research something worth thinking twice about: anecdotal information (i.e., a story) raises more than twice as much money as statistical information (i.e., data). And here's an unfortunate surprise: if you mix stories and statistics, giving won't improve.

Statistics and stories speak to different parts of the brain. Stories speak to the spendthrift part (the frontal lobes). Statistics speak to the cheapskate part (the jelly in the middle of the brain donut). Once the cheapskate part is awakened, the spendthrift part tends to slink away, bullied by reason. "Is that charity really worth *all* that much money?" the cheapskate brain asks. And asks. And asks. Crazy, huh? Numbers kill response. Yet it's that simple.

Flaw #8: The newsletter isn't set up for rapid skimming. I subscribe to three daily newspapers; two of them offer me America's best journalism, while the other's for local news. And yet I efficiently absorb the gist, well over 100,000 words daily, in less than half an hour.

How do I perform this amazing feat? I look at headlines, pull quotes, photos and captions—all the bigger, bolder, briefer stuff—searching for news that interests me. Like most people (research shows), I rarely read past the first paragraph of any article.

If you tell your readers important stuff in paragraph 3, you can safely assume that almost no one saw it.

Flaw #9: Your newsletter has weak or dysfunctional headlines. If any fatal flaw deserves the title "Most Deadly," this is it. Headlines are a key reader convenience.

And if you don't accept my nine flaws, maybe you'll trust Bob Ball . . . .

In a March 2012 Masterworks blog entry, Bob Ball—like Jeff Brooks, a hyper-skilled Domain Group alum—lists the principles behind the extraordinary success of "Jubilee," a donor newsletter produced by Prison Fellowship, a faith-based child and family assistance charity.

Bob Ball lists "10 principles" that yield surprising levels of gifts for Prison Fellowship's newsletter:

- Write the to the donor, for the donor, about the donor

- Ensure a high "you" quotient

- Touch the heart with a strong emotion

- Surprise and delight

- Appreciate the donor

- Design for readability

- Motivate another gift

- Make it convenient to give

- Appeal to the "Joy of Giving"

What to fix first . . . .

You have nine fatal flaws to avoid. But three are especially dangerous. These flaws are *extra*-fatal. If you don't fix these, your donor newsletter probably won't—can't, really—succeed.

The extra-fatal flaws are:

#1—An absence of "you." To keep their emotional attention, you have to repeatedly address readers directly, using the pronoun "you" and its cousins. Pay special attention to the headlines. Put a lot of you's there. Flagrant use of the word "you" is how you add emotional "stickiness" to your pages. It isn't inescapable stickiness, but it's the best there is.

#2—Does not use emotional triggers. Recent neuroscience is quite clear on this point: emotions drive response. Fear. Love. Duty. Faith. Anger. Guilt. A desire to pay back. A desire to pay forward. Swiss psychotherapist Carl Jung laid down the law: "There can be no transforming . . . of apathy into movement without emotion."

#9—Inept headlines. I've reviewed hundreds of charity newsletters over the last decade. Maybe 10 boasted truly functional headlines. The rest? "Rubbish," as Brits and Aussies love to say. Without functional headlines—i.e, the kind that meet basic journalistic criteria (you'll see what those are in following chapters)—your newsletter is simply incapable of injecting messages into donors' minds. Without "real" headlines, your newsletter is born to fail as a communications attempt.

So . . . before you tackle other flaws in your newsletter, *fix your mode of address . . . keep the emotions on boil . . . and fix your headlines.*

CHAPTER 17

Fatal Flaw #1:
Failing the "You" Test

*Y*ou.

Who would guess that a pronoun so common and small is in fact among the most powerful words in English?

Not internal-combustion-engine powerful, either, mind you. *Atomic* powerful, blazing-surface-of-the-sun powerful.

Who would guess that this mere monosyllable is the *most profitable word* in English-language fundraising?

It's true. Every day, effective use of the tiny word *you* moves mountains of cash into the bank accounts of nonprofit organizations.

How?

Because the word *you* wields a peculiar superpower. By itself, the word *you* can *force* people to pay attention. It's not like any other pronoun. It is truly in a class by itself: unlike other pronouns, *you* is an emotional trigger.

"Why?" you beg to know.

Have you forgotten your inner lab rat? Throughout our earliest, most impressionable years, legions of adults in authority (parents, relatives, teachers, rabbis, nuns, coaches, you name it) tell us what to do. They direct us, using the word "you" and our names ("Mr. Ahern, will you please face forward!") as their primary methods of control.

The truth is, for many of us over time (as the advertising industry knows quite well), the word *you* becomes far more than "just" a pronoun. It becomes a profound emotional trigger. Like the ringing bell that led Pavlov's dogs to salivate, the word *you* becomes what's called a "conditioned response."

You is glue; it literally is. It *sticks* the reader to the page.

Direct mail guru, Jerry Huntsinger, includes just one pronoun among his hand-selected list of "the 13 strongest words in English."

That word is *you.*

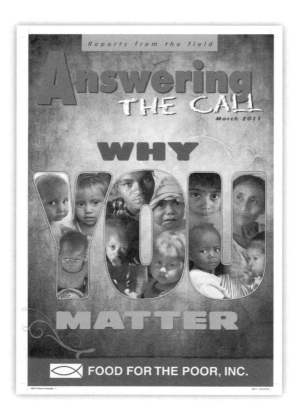

Food for the Poor's communications-savvy executive director, Angel Aloma, has turned his organization's newsletter into a powerhouse of donor-centricity. As you can see from this cover, it passes the "you" test with flying colors. *(Reprinted with Permission)*

You is as personal as newsletters get

Everyone knows that personalization in direct mail appeals ("Dear Jane Joyaux . . ." vs. "Dear Friend . . .") increases response rates and income.

There is probably only one kind of personalization your newsletter can easily indulge in: unlimited use of the word *you*.

The "you" test to the rescue

Perform the "you" test on every fundraising piece you write. I do. This test has saved me many times from sending out stuff that was "built to fail."

The "you" test is simplicity itself.

Get out a red pen. Circle each instance where you've used the word *you* or any variation thereof (*yours, yourself, you're*).

Then squint. Are there lots of red circles . . . or very few? Or are there red circles everywhere you look—at the top, at the bottom, in the middle, and *especially* in your headlines?

If so, you've passed the "you" test with flying colors.

But don't be complacent. I evaluate hundreds of nonprofit publications and websites in a year. Most of them badly fail the "you" test.

CHAPTER 18

Fatal Flaw #2: Lack of Emotional Triggers

Direct mail is without doubt the most heavily tested communications medium in the world.

Over the decades, fundraisers and other direct marketers have spent untold billions of dollars on tests. Serious direct mailers (i.e., the ones making good money at it) see every catalog, fundraising solicitation, or special offer as an opportunity to increase response and income, by testing something.

Over the decades, the direct mail industry has isolated a handful of "emotional triggers" that are reliably effective at improving response. They are, in alphabetical order: anger, exclusivity, flattery, fear, greed, guilt, and salvation.

Most will seem obvious.

"Exclusivity" means you're being offered membership in a special group: "Join the President's Circle."

"Salvation" means you're being offered a chance to match your deeds to your highest values or aspirations: "Help the poor; Jesus would approve" is salvation.

Negative and positive emotions work together

You might be thinking, "But these emotional triggers sound so negative!"

Not really. Every negative emotion has a powerful, positive flipside.

And somewhere between a negative emotion (fear) and a positive emotion (caring, compassion, duty, faith, hope, love) a check gets written or a gift is made online.

Here's a formula that works: stir a negative emotion; offer relief through a positive emotion; then invite the donor to help you right the wrong. Examples of this formula:

- "How early can you predict a child's future? A third-grader who can't read well will probably always be poor, studies show. The shame is, it doesn't have to happen. Our programs have poor kids reading well by first grade. We're ready to expand. Are you ready to help?"

- "Well-funded timber interests are cutting Congress down to size. But it's not too late to save America's wilderness. The fate of our last virgin forests now depends on you: your voice, your love of all things natural . . . and your strong support."

- "If you care about your personal freedom, there are seven new federal laws you're going to hate. The good news: There's still time to reverse them . . . if you'll stand with us today."

Emotional triggers battle inertia

People encountering the notion of emotional triggers for the first time sometimes object: "This is just a form of manipulation. I don't like being manipulated. And I certainly don't want to manipulate anyone else, no matter how worthy my cause."

Let's be clear: the biggest problem you'll encounter in fundraising isn't that someone falls prey to your magical, Svengali-like powers of persuasion. Your biggest problem will always be inertia.

INERTIA!!! It's the most powerful force on earth, more powerful than gravity. You get up on your soapbox, make your plea, and no one does a thing. That's real life. Most of the people you're trying to move will not act.

But when you use emotions wisely you can overcome some (never all) of that inertia. One more comment (and it's tough love): A working knowledge of emotional triggers is a prerequisite in effective communications. If you want to succeed at a professional level, you *have* to understand this stuff.

Too much "happy face"

Recently, a brand-name child development charity asked me to evaluate its donor communications.[1]

I visited its website first. What greeted me on the home page? Eleven children's faces from around the globe . . . and all were smiling. Big smiles, too, on pretty clean faces; not an apparent care in the world. One boy held a goat, and even the goat seemed to be smiling. (Goats come with a built-in grin, a farmer later explained.)

This mistake is perfectly understandable. In their eagerness to demonstrate effectiveness, charities sometimes cross a line. They show lots of great results. But they neglect to show much ongoing need.

The charity assumes all those happy faces broadcast a positive message, "We're doing great work here!" But at the same time you might be inadvertently telling your readers something quite discouraging. Those same smiling faces can also say to donors, "Job's done. And you're not needed."

In a donor newsletter, you need "need"—a need for help.

Create a small evil rip in the universe that only your newsletter readers can mend. They will thank you for that opportunity with their gifts, because helping others is emotionally satisfying.

Postscript

If you asked me to pick the top three emotional states I hope donors experience each time they receive any organization's newsletter, it would be these:

- I was **smart** for investing in this charity.

- I am **needed**.

- I am **useful** (i.e., important).

How do you nurture these three emotions?

---

1 Think you're not a charity? I beg to differ. If you're asking people to give you money, you're a charity . . . whether you're Harvard, the Mayo Clinic, Greenpeace . . . or the local food bank.

Got emotion? Food for the Poor does. Those are real tears on a real face in this plea for help.
(Reprinted with Permission)

Your readers will feel smart if you're reporting success, thanks to their gifts. Your readers will feel needed if you make it quite clear that there is still work for them to do. Your readers will feel useful if YOU TELL THEM SO! And only if.

CHAPTER 19

An Irresistible Emotional Trigger: Flattery. Even if You're Faking It. (PS: You Won't Need to.)

The human brain likes flattery.

Flattery is a "never fail" strategy.

That's *not* my opinion, I hasten to add: it's neuroscience. Brain chemistry.

Even flattery *that I know for sure is **false*** leaves "a lasting and positive impression of the flatterer," as the respected *Neuromarketing* blog reported in 2010. Turns out, human brains cannot tell the difference between the good stuff and the fake.

Flattery will get you nowhere, the axiom insists. That's a lie.

In truth, it's just the opposite: flattery takes you far.

I've never had to fake flattery when writing to donors, I want to add. The thought of someone taking the risk to trust my cause with their hard-earned cash fills me with admiration and humility.

CHAPTER 20

Fatal Flaw #9: Bad Headlines

Pop quiz.

Which is more important: The headline? Or the article?

You might reasonably assume the article is the star. It took ages to research and write. It's packed with information. It's long.

But not so fast. Think about it: no one reads an article who wasn't first lured in by a headline, right? When you encounter the news each day, online or in the paper, you make your initial reading decisions entirely based on headlines, photos, and other *summary* bits of information that lead you into the article.

Not sure? Well, you do: research says you do. According to recent data from the Poynter Institute, the majority of people read the headlines . . . and pretty much *only* the headlines. Fewer than one in five (less than 20 percent) read beyond the opening paragraph or so of any article. The loneliest language on the planet is in paragraph four: almost no one ever visits.

In our time-pressed, over-messaged world, people prefer to grab-and-go. A headline's plenty, thank you.

So the correct answer to the pop quiz is this: in terms of numbers of readers reached, headlines matter more—in fact they matter far, *far* more—than the stories that follow them.

There's money in being the rare charity that does this well

Only a negligible minority of your donors will ever read beyond the headline of any story you shove in front of them.

That's the truth. It'll never change. It will only get worse, as our attention spans are jack-hammered by the Internet and social media.

So work with it. In fact, take advantage of it, because writing efficient, effective headlines will distinguish *your* organization from the many organizations that don't have this skill.

I've reviewed hundreds of charity newsletters over the last decade. Maybe 10 of them had functional headlines. The rest—hundreds—didn't, which means they were literally born to fail.

Without "real" headlines, the kind that meet basic journalistic criteria, your newsletter is simply incapable of injecting messages into donors' minds.

So . . . before you tackle other flaws in your newsletter, *fix your headlines*.

You have my sympathies. I imagine that when you decided to pursue fundraising as a profession, you did not expect headline writing would be an essential skill you had to master. But it is . . . if you want your newsletter to succeed. If you cannot write a good headline, you cannot publish an effective newsletter; and there is no Plan B.

The true purpose of headlines

It's a given: your messages must penetrate via your headlines, if they're going to penetrate at all.

Therefore, it's also a given that you must write effective headlines, or your newsletter will be a waste of time and money. Three points . . . .

- Headlines are NOT just the bigger type at the top of the article.

- Headlines have a demanding and very specific job in journalism. That job is to *summarize the story* in as few words as possible, so readers can at a glance decide whether they want to read any deeper. If readers are interested in what the headline is about, they might stay or come back later. If they're not interested, they immediately move on to the next headline.

- Reading headlines is one of the things that separates humans from other animals. We take in information "simply" by skimming words. Words that are *easy to visualize* as images or little moving pictures penetrate the deepest and the fastest. "Interdisciplinary" (hard to visualize) will never light up my brain like "red" (easy to visualize).

Headlines are a reader convenience, first and foremost.

"Well-written headlines are the main entry point to text," Dr. Mario R. Garcia points out in his book, *Redesigning Print for the Web*; he is an international authority on newspaper design. "A good headline [has] enticing words, good action verbs, the best possible summary of what the content is about, and, if possible, a surprise or 'hook' that pulls us in."

What NON-headlines look like

In the special case of donor newsletters, the headline has, in fact, *two* main jobs:

- To summarize the story; and

- To flood the reader's mind with joy.

Here is a sampling of front-page "headlines" ripped from real (or, to be honest, *attempted*) donor newsletters (and I wasn't trying to be mean when I made my selections):

- Strategic Plan on the Move

- A Word from Our Executive Director

- East Side Initiates NRZ

- An Inclusive Approach to Excellence

- Leadership Institute

- The Value of Volunteering

- Adoption Works!

- A Message from Jim Franklin, Gift Planning Counselor

Read that list again—only this time pretend you're a donor.

Of each headline, ask yourself a fundamental question: "Do I know *exactly* what this story is about?"

Then ask yourself a second question, just as fundamental, "Do I *care* what this story is about? Why is this story relevant to me?"

Stumped? Confused? Frustrated? You should be. The list contains nothing but dysfunctional (though common enough) nonprofit headlines. In the real world, they all earned an "F."

- **Their failure #1:** I cannot confidently say what the article which follows any of these headlines is *specifically* about. "Strategic Plan on the Move"? Moving where? A hundred different articles could just as easily squeeze beneath those 5 words. Moving up? Down? Fast? Slow? Drifting . . . or on target?

- **Their failure #2:** I don't know why I, the donor, should care.

Let us revisit communication's most primal law, the one built into every spinal column: "If you want to interest me, talk about me. Don't talk about you (i.e., the organization). *I* (not you) fascinate me. Your organization remains relevant to me because of what you say . . . *about me*.

"Are you telling me that I'm wise? Am I generous, you say? Am I caring? Am I spiritual? Am I good? Am I helping? Am I important?"

Hence, a professionally written headline for a donor newsletter will accomplish three things:

1. Clearly explain the gist of the story.

2. Include a hook that makes the story worth reading (something new, different, intriguing; it can be just a single word, used like dynamite).

3. Give your donors some (or all the) credit for the accomplishment reported in the story. That dose of flattery provides the emotional gratification that all donors (including me) crave.

The "Big Hand" test

How will you know—really *know*—if your headline is functional or dysfunctional?

Easy: ask a pal.

Put your headline in front of someone who has no idea what you're writing about. Do NOT show them the article. "Read the headline," you'll instruct them. "Tell me what this article is about, from the headline alone."

If a person of normal intelligence cannot give you a clear answer, then you MUST rewrite the headline.

Time management

Are you now spending hours writing your articles . . . and just a few minutes writing your headlines?

Reverse that habit. Spend real quality time writing your headlines. The articles you can kind of toss off, since very few people will ever read past the opening couple of paragraphs.

Write your headlines, in fact, as if the articles were printed in invisible ink . . . and all your eggs were in the headline basket.

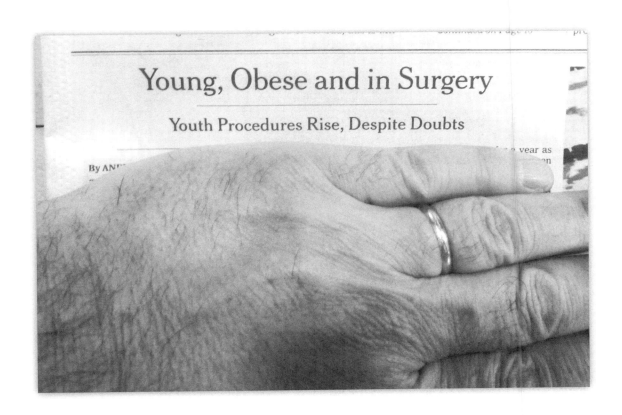

The "Big Hand" test in action. I've covered the article with my hand. The only information visible is the headline. Yet I know what these articles from the *New York Times* are about. These headlines PASS the test. Headlines that do NOT pass the Big Hand test are worthless junk and MUST be rewritten.

CHAPTER 21

A Model Headline

"Is Your Baby Racist?" the cover of *Newsweek* asked. There was a deck, too: "Exploring the Roots of Discrimination."
Now *there's* a headline. Let me count the ways . . . .

Way #1: It began with a powerful emotional hook.

"Is *my* baby racist? Say what?!?" This headline is an open challenge to the presumptions of every proud parent. Headlines are the baited fishing hooks of journalism: they reel readers in.

Way #2: It told me just enough so I understood roughly what the article was about.

I understood it was about babies. I understood it was about a surprising new truth. I understood it was about getting to the bottom of one of humankind's most discouraging, wasteful and violent tendencies: racism.

Newsweek's 2009 cover story explored new research from the University of Texas. Neuroscientists there had found the human brain has a built-in-at-birth biological predisposition toward judging people based on skin color: the color we are is the color we instinctively like and trust.

In post-slavery, racially polarized America, this was disturbing news. And yet a relief, too: maybe we're *all* racist, and we come by it naturally. Maybe racism isn't an individual failing; but a common, biologically-grounded problem we need to overcome.

Newsweek's headline is a mere nine words long. It runs over a close-up, life-size, full-color photo of a newly-minted Caucasian infant with huge beautiful eyes and an irrefutably innocent expression.

Is a picture truly worth a thousand words, as the saying goes? Well, here's the proof. The juxtaposition of jarring headline and flawless baby face was brilliant . . . and spoke volumes.

Now for the lesson. Please note: the headline has two parts. And each part plays a role. As published, it looked something like this:

Is Your Baby Racist?

Exploring the Roots of Discrimination

Two statements, typeset in different sizes.

The second line of the headline—"Exploring the Roots of Discrimination"—is known in journalism as a "deck."

Barbara G. Ellis, author of *The Copy-Editing and Headline Handbook*, defines "deck" as "a subordinate head that follows a newspaper's main headline." A main headline and its deck act as one unit, to be read at a glance. Together, they give the reader just enough information to either:

1. Stop me in my tracks, because *I must learn more* about this fascinating topic; or

2. Allow me to confidently *move on* with my life, because I know this particular story doesn't interest me.

Way #3: **It included the most profitable word in the English language.**

One teensy word leads to billions of dollars in consumer sales every year in North America, the UK, Australia and other English-speaking markets: the pronoun "you," in any of its variations (you, your, you're, yours).

I've said it before. I say it again: you is glue. The word "you" draws readers in and keeps them reading. The word "you" makes the story personal. The word "you" in a headline makes the story obviously about me, the reader.

Way #4: **It asked a question.**

Among professional direct mail copywriters, questions are known as "involvement devices." They're popular gimmicks because they deliver good results. Copywriters know that a headline posing a question will reliably cause more people to linger. After all, our brains are built to be curious. Questions in headlines simply take advantage of that fact.

It's said that Mozart's father used to waken young Wolfgang by playing a scale on the piano . . . all except the last note. Dad would deliberately leave the scale unresolved. And the boy genius couldn't stand it. He'd throw off his bed covers, rush to the keyboard, and finish the scale, adding that last satisfying note. A question can act the same way on your readers. A question can create a state of tension that requires resolution: "I must know the answer!"

Way #5: **It had news value. I.e., it surprised me.**

- Tell me stuff I already know or assume: I will ignore you.

- Tell me stuff I do NOT already know or assume: I will sit up straight and pay attention.

CHAPTER 22

How to Write Great Headlines

This is a charity headline that raised money:

Feeling the pinch: Overcrowding becomes Club's #1 issue

Followed by two subheads:

Popular programs, sharp increase in city's youth population fill Club to overflowing

New Teen Center planned . . . but tight money slows renovations

Thousands of dollars in new contributions came in prompted by this headline.

The Copy-Editing and Headline Handbook offers this simple headline formula: "[The] bedrock of masterly head writing . . . is that you write a short sentence summing up the story and then delete the extra words—like a telegram." Good advice: summarize and be concise.

But not too concise.

Unless you're reporting *Titanic Sinks*, it's unlikely your summary will pack down into just a couple of words.

I have on my desk an issue of *The Wall Street Journal*. There are four front-page feature stories. The average length of their headlines is 25 words, if you count the head, the kicker and the deck together.

"Headline I know. But *kicker* and *deck?*"

You might be unfamiliar with the terms "kicker" and "deck." Let me show you what I'm referring to, with this example pulled from a donor newsletter:

Knock, knock. Who's there?
Kids who want to study!

Up 177%: Demand soars for Club's free afterschool homework program

Project Learn turns "C" students into "B" students

The "knock, knock" line is *the kicker*. A kicker is a fragmentary bit of text above the headline. It's also called in the trade an *eyebrow*: it winks at you. Kickers flirt, tease, hint. It's typeset in a small point size.

The "Up 177%" line is *the headline*. It's typeset in a large point size.

The "Project Learn" line is *the deck*. That's its official term in journalism. It's typeset in a point size that's smaller than the headline but larger than the article. You can have more than one deck, incidentally. I've run stories with up to four decks.

Kickers are optional. Decks are indispensable.

Headlines and decks really work together as a single unit. One tells the tale. The other comments on the tale. Journalism guru Ann Wylie offers these guidelines:

- Use the headline to telegraph a single, newsworthy story in eight words or less.

- Add information in a deck of 14 words or less. Take a different view. Do not repeat the same information as the headline.

- In the first sentence of your first paragraph, you answer two questions: "What happened?" and "Why should the reader care?"

An observation: 99 out of 100 nonprofit newsletters I see don't use decks at all. That's a big wasted opportunity . . . because anyone who reads a headline will probably read the deck, too. Few will read the article itself.

The verb *is* the story

Here's a list of headline verbs plucked from *The Wall Street Journal*:

blames	spark
clash	sputters
mauled	surge
devour	reject
embrace	threaten
looms	

And here is a random list of headline verbs pulled from nonprofit newsletters:

administer	reach
benefits	sets
establishes	shares
help	unifies
listed	visits
plan	

The difference is striking.

The nonprofit list is mostly safe, unexciting, deflated, or stiff. Few of the nonprofit verbs evoke a scene. They don't stimulate the senses.

The Wall Street Journal verbs, on the other hand, are highly sensory. You can see them ("devour," "looms," "surge," "mauled"). You can even *hear* them ("sputters," "clash").

Ann Wylie advises, "When it comes to your headline, the verb *is* the story. The sexier the verb, the sexier the story." She cites former Esquire editor, Byron Dobell, who wisely said: "A story should be a verb, not a noun."

CHAPTER 23

What is News?

News is available to us 24 hours a day. We swim in it. It renews us. It exhausts us. And yet what is it, exactly? What actually counts as news?

News is any information that (1) is fresh and (2) interests the target reader.

The fresh part is easy: it's anything I haven't heard before. It might be completely new information. Or it might be a new chapter of an ongoing story: "Three years ago we introduced you to Annitah. Her outlook was grim then. We want you to see how far she's come since, thanks to your help!"

The interest part is easy, too. Stock investors want updates about the companies they trade. Voters want updates about the candidates they're considering. And donors—your target audience—want updates about the missions they've invested in.

Where do you find news?

News originates on the front lines, where the mission is on boil: from the social workers dealing with the "new normal" of persistent high unemployment; from the professors blazing new trails in the laboratories of a research university; from the artistic director struggling to find a local audience for revolutionary theatre; from the grateful patients whose lives were saved in your hospital.

Learn to be a "news spotter."

- **Look for anecdotes that typify a problem your organization tries to remedy:** "A year ago, Julia Smith could afford a cozy apartment for her and her middle-school daughter. Today, they live in a rusted car. And yet there's hope."

- **Look for trends, because trends are by definition news:** "A 25% increase in customers at the Food Bank? Hunger in Houston hasn't been this bad for decades, manager reveals."

- **Look for surprising, even shocking, information:** "Baby spiders thrive in mom's loving care . . . unless she's hungry, notes zoo keeper."

- **Look for emerging problems donors can help you fix:** "Dust to dust? Not so fast. A new donor-supported restoration lab at the museum could turn back the clock on our fading masterpieces."

- **Look for new angles on favorites:** "Peeved hummingbirds add buzz to popular aviary. Here's a tip: Don't wear red hats."

Eschew filler

Do donors need to know about your planning retreat and who attended? Doubtful. Do donors care about staff changes? Not much, not really (although to your face they'll be polite). What about new board members? Few donors care.

A donor newsletter packed with this kind of low-wattage stuff has adverse consequences. You're training your target audience to ignore you. The subliminal message that accumulates quickly, over a couple of worthless issues: "Nothing important here."

Donors care first and foremost about results. They care about the mission: Was it advanced? With every new issue they want to know one thing: "How have supporters like me saved/changed/improved the world since the last time you sent me this newsletter?"

CHAPTER 24

Making News Out of Thin Air

Hey, it happens. Sometimes there's not enough real news to fill an issue. Here are four, fast ways to brew up "news-like" material that donors will find interesting.

Fact vs. Myth (a.k.a. the Reality Check)

A "Fact vs. Myth" column uses some of your vast insider knowledge to inform and entertain the donor. Here's an excerpt from the Clean Water Action (MI) newsletter:

> *MYTH: Property owners cannot maintain their beaches without getting in trouble with the MI Department of Environmental Quality (MDEQ) or the Army Corps of Engineers (ACOE).*
>
> FACT: [Here are] highlights of what property owners can do without any permits from the ACOE or MDEQ—build sand castles; hand shovel/manually rake dead fish, zebra mussel shells, trash and dead vegetation; manually bury debris such as dead fish and dead vegetation; bonfire building; temporary tent building and camping by permission of the property owner; and beaching boats and seasonal storage of ice shanties.

The preceding myth-and-fact might or might not interest you, but it was well chosen for its target audience: lakeshore property owners. It delivers useful information about what they can and cannot do. It reduces worry and helps keep people out of trouble with the law. It also positions Clean Water Action as a fair-minded organization that isn't anti-owner, despite occasional disagreements on specific issues.

The Update

Updates help position your organization as an authority in your field, something that's probably high on your list of goals. All kinds of support (donor, policymaker, media) gravitate toward a recognized authority.

"West Nile Virus: One Year Later" is a perfect example of the authoritative update. The headline appears on the front cover of *Conservator*, the member magazine of Ducks Unlimited Canada. The mission of Ducks Unlimited Canada: saving wildfowl by preserving wetlands. The news value of this article: the appearance of a deadly mosquito, which adds a surprising downside to the mission of wetlands conservation.

The List

"Top Ten." "Seven Worst." "Three Most."

"There's something irresistibly attractive about lists," says Andy Goodman in his newsletter, *Free-range thinking*. "Whether scratched on paper as reminders of tasks that need to be done today, or etched in stone as moral guidelines"—oh, right, the Ten Commandments—"lists have a unique way of taking the complex and making it orderly and understandable. The media inundate us with lists—of box office leaders, top performing stocks, sexiest men alive—precisely because editors recognize their consistent appeal."

The National Parks Conservation Association (NPCA) annually releases a list naming the "Ten Most Endangered National Parks." The press loves it. So do NPCA's 800,000+ donors and dues-paying members. NPCA's "Ten Most Endangered" gives them a powerful reason to continue giving. The list distills the mission down into one bracing shot of anger and fear, reminding everyone of what's at stake and the urgency.

The "Did You Know?"

Here's an example from the Conservation Law Foundation newsletter: "Did you know? . . . as over 100 power plants remained shut down on the second day of the Northeast's massive blackout, visibility increased by as much as 20 miles because the concentration of light-scattering particles caused by sulfur dioxide emissions was reduced by 70 percent."

Donors to the Conservation Law Foundation hope to save New England's environment from further degradation. This particular "Did you know?" posted prominently on the newsletter's front page, reminds donors exactly what they're fighting for and what their gifts hope to achieve: a day when pollution doesn't add a dangerous haze to the very air they breathe.

CHAPTER 25

"Just Add Water" Article Ideas

No idea what to write? The ever-helpful Kivi Leroux Miller offers this checklist:

- How-to Articles
- Advice Columns
- First-Person Anecdotes
- Trends
- News Roundups
- Reviews
- Recommendations
- Success Stories
- Personal Profiles

- Lists (e.g. Top Ten)
- Legislative Updates
- Action Alerts
- Hot Finds
- Wish Lists
- Sponsors/Partners
- Surveys/Research Results
- Fact v. Fiction

Kivi also offers some standard headlines you can resort to if you're having a "less than imaginative" day (join the club):

- The Secret of [blank]
- Get Rid of [problem] Once and For All
- [Do something] like [world-class example]
- Have a [or] Build a [blank] You Can Be Proud Of
- The Lazy [blank's] Way to [blank]
- Do You Recognize the [number] Early Warning Signs of [blank]?
- You Don't Have to Be [something challenging] to Be [desired result]

on counselling..
(...nued from front page)

...his is not just about ...risoners...this is about ...milies, the community, ...e whole nation. The more ...eople that get help here, ...e less crime there is ...oing to be on the outside, ...e less victims, the ...appier families. It's a ...pple effect."

...dds, "No two clients are ...me. You have to be able to ...o John, aged 50, and Joe, ...20, with different histories. ...s, alcohol, poverty, abuse, ...ployment, peer pressure. I try ...ow them they can take control ...They get that bit of belief in ...selves, and you can see the ...ting. I don't think people ...e how decent these men and ...en are – they just got caught ...th the wrong thing at the ...g time."

...ing demand

...are referred to MQI for ...son counselling as part of their ...assessment. But as word ...ds, more and more seek the ...hemselves. Says Team Leader ...It wasn't long before we had ...'s demand in the prisons."

The far-reaching effect of your donations –

Factbox: How MQI's Prison Work & Rehab Pays Off

€70,000:
cost to the state to accommodate one prisoner in 2010[1]

€32,517:
average cost of crime for a dependent drug user if they are not in treatment[3]

Three-fold:
the savings on drug treatment over the money spent on criminal justice alone[2]

10,293:
total in-prison drugs counselling sessions provided by MQI in 2011

Nearly 8 out of 10:
people who successfully complete MQI's High Park drug free treatment programme, funded in part thanks to your support

[1]Irish Prison System, 2010 Annual Report
[2]British Home Office study
[3]National Treatment Agency for Substance Misuse (UK), 2012

---

rarely get to the top of our waiting list. At the bigger prisons, it's even tougher. We have such little windows of opportunity to help, where someone is only in for a month or two. Being able to reach is not just about prisoners alone. This is about the entire prison and the staff, the families, the community, the whole nation. The more people that get help here, the less crime there is going

---

MQI's Factbox is a perfect example of "non-breaking" news. What qualifies as "news"? News is anything the reader doesn't already know. Here, on page 3 of the Quay newsletter, donors quickly learn from a highly skimmable list-in-a-box just how well they've invested in their charity. Writer: Lisa Sargent. Designer: Sandie Collette. *(Reprinted with Permission)*

CHAPTER 26

What a Front Page is For

Thought experiment:

You pick up today's edition of *The New York Times*. The cover features the lunch menus for various public schools in the Big Apple . . . plus some junior high school ball scores . . . and that's it for front page news.

Just imagine . . . .

Imagine if *your* daily newspaper suddenly devoted its front page to IN-significant news—instead of the most pressing news. You'd think the editors had lost their professional minds—*and you'd be right!* You'd find a better paper.

It wasn't a "thought experiment"—it was the truth

Yet . . . many—maybe most—donor newsletters I see suffer from exactly that problem.

They do NOT report what donors really care about (and crave). Instead, doggedly, issue after issue into the indefinite future, charities repeatedly squander their best chance of persuading a donor on an anemic front page.

As they say: You never get a second chance to make a first impression. Waste your most important real estate—the front page—on stuff that doesn't matter to your donors, and you'll quickly train them to ignore your publication.

Donors are interested in what you did with their money (i.e., how you advanced the mission), what you *could* do with their money (i.e., your vision of the great things you could do), and whether their money mattered ("Thanks, donors, for a job well done!"). There's only one right answer to the question, "Did my gift matter?" That answer: "It mattered a lot. Every gift, no matter what the amount, matters. Every gift allows us to do more."

Case in point: the front-page essay "From the desk of . . . ." the ED, the board chair, the founder.

I once had about 70 donor newsletters spread out around my office. I was evaluating them as a "species," looking for common elements. The only things they had in common, I was surprised to see, were two things that doomed them to sure failure.

First, the "headlines" were mostly not real headlines at all. They were just big type.

Second, and more to the point of this chapter, about 70 percent of them wasted their front page real estate on a yawn-inducing essay "From the Executive Director's Desk." Please note: I'm not suggesting a ban on "From the desk of . . ." columns. They have their place. Usually, though, it's not on the front page.

How Pastor John made money

Years ago when we met, Pastor John (John R. Bohnsack) was executive director of the Community Emergency Service in Minneapolis.

His humble, compassionate, and uplifting "Director's Discourse" columns filled every front page of the organization's monthly newsletter.

In a simple, conversational style, he told stories about people who needed help. He talked about how easy it was to change a life. He used the magic word *you* over and over. He called his readers "friend" and meant it.

Pastor John used emotional triggers like greed, salvation, and duty quite openly: "God does seem to find ways of returning tenfold and sometimes even one-hundredfold to those who reach out in faith and give through this ministry to folks whose spirits have been drenched by catastrophe."

And it worked. His "Director's Discourse" inspired an outpouring of money, thousands of dollars a month, to help the city's hungry and homeless.

But Pastor John is the exception.

CHAPTER 27

The "Inverted Pyramid" (i.e., Put the Important Stuff First)

One of the staples of journalism is a story structure known as the "inverted pyramid." Why the name? Because the story starts in the middle of the action and works its way toward the point.

Here's how it works:

1. You start with what happened.

2. Then you explain *why* it happened.

3. Last, you add commentary and other interesting, but not necessarily essential, background.

Here's the story of the three little pigs, told in inverted pyramid style:

> "A wooden home in Pleasantville was reduced to matchsticks last night when a long-standing feud between a wolf and a family of bachelor pigs erupted into violence. A police spokesperson said feuds of this kind are 'predictable occurrences between natural enemies.' A neighbor said, 'I warned those pigs to build with brick.'"

Get to the point . . . fast

The inverted pyramid is an ancient editorial convenience. If space is tight, a news editor can simply trim paragraphs off the bottom of the story, safe in knowing the really important information is at the top.

But that's probably not why you want the inverted pyramid in your bag of tricks. You'll want it handy because you're painfully aware that almost no one reads past the first paragraph. The point of your story ("See what we've accomplished with your gift!") must be right up front—or there's a very real risk readers will miss it.

Do NOT slowly reveal your surprises. Your good news isn't a gift to be unwrapped. Putting key points in the second, third or subsequent paragraphs will merely cause many donors to miss those points completely.

When the leader of an outside accreditation team concludes that yours is "the best daycare center I've ever seen," don't hide that incredible accomplishment at the *end* of 250 other words (as one newsletter did). SHOUT IT!!! LOUD!!! IMMEDIATELY!!!

CHAPTER 28

Most People Skim. Few Read Deep.

Watch your own behavior next time you pick up the newspaper. You browse first. If you find something of interest, *then* you start reading. And even then, you often read no more than a paragraph or two before jumping to another story, unless you're enjoying a leisurely morning.

Same goes for donors. When your newsletter arrives, the first thing they do is browse: skim a few headlines, look at the photos, maybe read a caption, to see if anything's of interest. If nothing is, they put the newsletter aside, likely never to return.

Which means, if you have nothing of interest in your "browser level" (see the list below), you've wasted your time and money.

Don't expect donors to read deep, because most of them won't. Instead of saying, "When people *read* our newsletter," start saying instead, "When people *skim* our newsletter, this is what they will learn."

What readers look at, science says

Siegfried Vögele, Dean of the Institute of Direct Marketing in Munich, Germany, electrified the direct marketing industry when he introduced his eye-motion research in the 1980s.

In his studies, Vögele used cameras to observe the human eye as it encountered a fresh printed page. He confirmed that our eyes tend to look first at the biggest splashes of ink (photos, headlines) and then at briefer, bolder things (captions, bullet lists, three-word paragraphs). Long copy—articles and such—is ignored until last.

A decade later, Drs. Mario Garcia and Pegie Stark Adam conducted the first Poynter Institute study using eye-tracking equipment. Their findings reinforced Vögele's:

- Photos attracted attention. Color photos were viewed as often as black and white. Color was a powerful tool that pulled the eye toward various parts of a page, especially when readers viewed two facing pages.

- Eyes followed a common pattern of navigation. The majority of readers entered all pages through the dominant photo or illustration, then traveled to the dominant headline, then to teasers and cutlines [captions], and finally to text.

- Teasers [pull quotes] accompanied by visuals received far more attention than text-only teasers.

- Two facing pages were viewed as one. When viewing two inside facing pages, readers entered the pages on the right hand side and traveled immediately left. Readers viewed a two-page spread as if it were one single unit.

- Readers love color. The majority of participants said they read more of the text on a colorful page, though, in fact, many had not. Color also gave readers the illusion that there was more information than appeared on the pages.

- Images (photos and graphics) were viewed more than text. Photos and artwork were looked at the most, followed by headlines and advertising, then briefs and cutlines. Text was read the least.

Why what you put on your "skimming level" is so important

I feel safe saying that no more than 20 percent of your so-called "readers" will ever penetrate much beyond the first sentence of any given article.

What are the other 80 percent doing? They're skimming. They're looking briefly at your "skimming level," comprised of . . .

- Photos and illustrations

- Headlines and decks

- Pull quotes (Poynter called them "teasers")

- Captions (Poynter called them "cutlines")

- Bullet lists

I.e., they're looking at anything that's easy and quick to read.

Successful publications are built backwards from the needs and wants of their target audience. The target audience for donor newsletters is, of course, donors. So . . . what do donors want and expect from the organization they've helped?

- Reports on how their donations are changing the world

- Appreciation, praise, and head-over-heels love

And . . . where will those messages and sentiments have the best chance of penetrating the largest number of "reader" brains?

NOT in the lengthy bits (articles).

Any message you hope to get across MUST be in the bigger, bolder, briefer bits (headlines, pull quotes, captions), the bits that people habitually skim.

On the left, a non-skimmable page. Why? Because the headline doesn't tell me enough to convey a full message. On the right, a skimmable page. Why? Because I can read the headline and absorb a message that's important to donors: "You are saving lives...."
(Reprinted with Permission)

On the left, a charity newsletter . . . as the charity sees it. On the right, the same newsletter . . . as the skimming reader sees it. Bottom line: don't invest too much hope in your articles, since very few people ultimately read them. Put your important messages in your headlines.

CHAPTER 29

Pull Quotes Bring Your Buried Treasures to Light

Even if you're not familiar with the term "pull quote," you're familiar with pull quotes themselves. You read them all the time, in newspapers and magazines. Pull quotes are an important reader convenience. As a reader, you use them all the time to decide at a glance whether or not you're interested in a story.

What is a pull quote? (A.k.a. drop out quote, pullout quote, breakout or blurb.)

Dr. Barbara G. Ellis defines it thus: "A key quote from a story that has been lifted and [often] set in 14- to 18-point type with rules or boxes. It is used to break up the grayness of text, as well as to attract readers into the story."

Let's look at a sharply wrought example of that second use.

It appeared in a long profile of a technology firm. The profile ran in a national business magazine trusted by investors. Here's the pull quote the editors chose:

"There's no way they'll become profitable,"
says one analyst. "I don't think they'll survive."

Imagine the scene. An investor, idly flipping the pages, quickly spots that pull quote. It is, after all, the only bigger, easy-to-read type on a page otherwise filled with dense gray text. And it warns, in no uncertain terms: *Red alert! Company in trouble!*

Instantly, the former idle flipper changes into an avid reader, to sniff out the name of this potential loser before it costs her money.

That's the power of a well-chosen pull quote. If it hooks your interest, it stops you cold.

Pull quotes to the rescue

A pull quote can single-handedly rescue *your* message from oblivion.

I'm looking at a page from a rape crisis center newsletter. It is carpeted wall-to-wall with an article, a carefully researched article that someone labored over. It says important things about the bizarre twists of domestic violence. But the article has three strikes against it:

1. It has a misleading (vague, meek, tossed-off) headline: "Some Challenges We Face." A headline like that could be about almost anything from aardvarks to zealots.

2. It starts sluggishly, beginning with a history lesson (yawn). "The anti-rape movement as documented in traditional histories and timelines is by all accounts less than thirty years old."

3. It is dense, *visually* dense, with paragraphs and sentences that run on for miles.

Yet . . . in this almost impenetrable article the author buries one amazing anecdote, an anecdote so shocking, so sickening it cries out for redress. If any donor ever read it.

But almost no one did. Why? Because that anecdote was buried 300 words deep, where virtually no one ever goes. I doubt five out of a thousand donors who received this newsletter ever read beyond the article's lecturing first words.

Which means they missed this red-hot poker:

. . . [our hotline] received a call from a woman who had not eaten anything but some slices of bread for days. Confined to a wheelchair, this woman [a paraplegic who could not unlock her chair] was starved by her husband, who would put food just out of her reach.

That brief but shocking anecdote is exactly the kind of story that brings the blood of true believers to a boil. And money flows from people on boil, if you ask them while they're hot. They're angry. They want to do something about this vile injustice right now. And your organization offers hope.

A pull quote would have saved that anecdote from oblivion. Repeating that anecdote as a pull quote, in big, bold type, would have brought it to the attention of countless more donors . . . and put its emotional treasure to work, inspiring your base with righteous anger.

Don't bury your best stuff. EXALT IT!!! . . . in pull quotes.

CHAPTER 30

The AP Formula for Captions

A caption is the "text describing a photograph or illustration," says *Desktop Publishing by Design*. Simple.

And every photo should have a caption. Otherwise, you leave readers guessing—which is *never* a good thing. Professional publications strive to keep their readers oriented (as opposed to disoriented) and fully informed (as opposed to mystified).

Here's a formula for the standard two-sentence caption, from *The Associated Press Stylebook and Libel Manual*:

- The first sentence . . . describes what the photo shows, in the present tense, and states where and when the photo was made.

- The second sentence . . . gives background on the news event or describes why the [subject of the] photo is significant.

That second sentence is where you slip in your message, by providing a context for the events or people or objects shown. The caption with the accompanying photo follows a different formula, especially suited to donor newsletters:

- The first sentence . . . describes the issue/problem illustrated by the photo.

- The second sentence . . . gives the donor credit for helping someone in need.

An evocative photo, but what's the story? Maybe something like this: "He moved here for a steady job . . . and found it. But housing locally is out of reach for normal salaries. While he waits for an affordable apartment to open up, he gratefully accepts our hospitality . . . *under a roof funded by your generosity.* **Your kindness means this man, this time, won't lose hope.** Thank you!" (*Used with permssion of the Manchester Area Conference of Churches*)

CHAPTER 31

Elements of a Skimmable Page

The diagram (accompanying this key) shows the full arsenal of easily skimmed typographic elements. It's quite likely that most people will skim these elements in the sequence shown here: eyebrow first, headline second, deck third and so forth.

1. **Eyebrow.** A little bit of type above the headline.

2. **Headline.** The biggest type on the page. Headlines summarize the gist of the article. If people decide to read an article, it's because of the headline. The headline is the ad for the article.

3. **Deck.** The deck provides commentary and insight. Decks and headlines work together as inseparable pairs to convey the full drama of the article.

4. **Caption [cutline].** Placed adjacent to the photo, a caption will benefit from the fact that 80 percent or more of your readers will look at the photos.

5. **Pull quote [teaser].** Technically, a pull quote is a verbatim statement extracted from the article and made bigger. It's meant to draw the reader in. Anything you choose to nominate for pull quote status should be of special interest to the donor. A big thank you is always good.

6. **Subhead.** Subheads are brief boldface statements that break up the gray mass of the article, making it look easier to read. Subheads help the reader leapfrog through the article by summarizing key points.

7. **Brief.** A small, related item given special graphic treatment. This brief offers donors an online video to view. Viewing videos, answering questionnaires, writing officials—any relevant action that donors can easily take—will help deepen their relationship

with your organization.

8. **Lead.** The first sentence or paragraph of an article is called a "lead" (rhymes with "heed"). The lead is special. Most people won't bother with the full article. But many will read the lead, because it comes first and has white space above it. A dull lead will suppress readership (starting with statistics is a predictable interest-killer, unless your donors are all sceintists or policy wonks). A lead that has me wondering "what happens next?" will drive readership up. Joseph Sugarman famously said, "The purpose of the first sentence is to get you to read the second sentence." But don't stop there. Read his entire book, *Advertising Secrets of the Written Word*. It's one of the most useful books on persuasion I know.

9. **Line length/column width.** Narrower columns help people speed read. The sample column is 55 characters wide, including spaces, using a 12-point Times New Roman typeface. This is about as wide as you want your column to be (and about as small as you want your type to be, for older eyes). The wider the column, the more often the skimming reader's eye gets lost, which is annoying. And annoyed readers don't stick around.

CHAPTER 32

What Wheildon Discovered (and Gutenberg Didn't)

It's hard enough to get someone to pay *any* attention. Don't make it even harder by adding visual labor: you *will* pay a price.

There are four ways newsletters typically add visual labor to the experience of reading articles on a printed page:

1. By printing the articles in colored type

2. By printing the articles over colored backgrounds or on non-white paper

3. By printing the articles in reverse type (i.e., white type on a black or dark background)

4. By printing the articles in sans serif type (Arial or Helvetica are the most common sans serif typefaces)

Some graphic designers reject these facts, so I've included a few bits of relevant data below.

Wheildon's science erases centuries of opinion

Colin Wheildon did the English-speaking world a profound favor.

Mr. Wheildon, a distinguished Australian magazine editor, began researching readability issues in the 1980s. He published a small-circulation, office-bound report.

Please understand: Colin Wheildon's research has had very limited circulation. Hundreds have read it—not tens of thousands. Hence, very few graphic designers within your ken know anything of Wheildon's research; I've yet to meet one who does.

Implausibly enough, Mr. Wheildon's research seems to be the first pure-science investigation regarding readability since Gutenberg introduced the printing press to Europe in the 1430s. Before Colin Wheildon ran his tests, readability had been a matter of "informed" opinion, accepted trade wisdom, and hearsay.

Colin Wheildon did his research so his advertisers could design better ads, among other things. But much of his research applies to any reading matter, including newsletters.

In the table that follows (reprinted with permission from Colin Wheildon), I've summarized some of his key findings. These are the ones I think you need to know about, to evaluate your newsletter's design.

Design choice	"How easy is it to comprehend?"		
Article in black ink on white paper	Good: 70%	Fair: 19%	Poor: 11%
Article in black ink on pale blue paper (= to a 30% tint of cyan)	Good: 38%	Fair: 19%	Poor: 43%
Article in black ink on white paper	Good: 70%	Fair: 19%	Poor: 11%
Article in purple ink on white paper	Good: 51%	Fair: 13%	Poor: 36%
Article in black on white background	Good: 70%	Fair: 19%	Poor: 11%
Article in white on black background (i.e., reverse type)	Good: 0%	Fair: 12%	Poor: 88%
Article in serif type	Good: 67%	Fair: 19%	Poor: 14%
Article in sans serif type	Good: 12%	Fair: 23%	Poor: 65%
Headlines in black	Good: 67%	Fair: 19%	Poor: 14%
Headlines in bright colors	Good: 17%	Fair: 18%	Poor: 65%
Headlines in dark colors	Good: 52%	Fair: 28%	Poor: 20%

Why reading *sans* serif type is slower than molasses

Colin Wheildon's research found that text set in sans serif type (Helvetica, Arial) is five times harder (slower) to comprehend than text set in serif type (Times New Roman, Garamond).

Why? Training.

In North America, in print, most of the time you read serif typefaces, not sans serif. Most newspapers, magazines, and books are set in serif type. Serif type is the default. (You can easily confirm this for yourself next time you visit a bookstore. Glance at a dozen books chosen at random. You'll see that most are typeset in a serif font.)

Your brain becomes accustomed to interpreting serif type at light speed. Sans serif type, on the other hand, is relatively uncommon. *Curve ahead!* Your brain finds these less-familiar sans serif letterforms harder to process quickly. Recognition slows down, and so does reading.

Bear in mind, this all has to do with the printed page. Websites are different. On the web, sans serif faces are far more common than serif faces. And so our "readability brains" learn: we train all the time on what is most common.

The missed opportunity? Campaigns build culture, and your culture is your future

You all know Aesop's fable, The Tortoise and the Hare. It's a race between unequal partners. Spoiler alert: the Tortoise wins. Because the Tortoise is focused, resolute, and follows a better strategic plan, written in part by a reputable consultant.

Capital campaigns are peculiarly good at building the culture of philanthropy. When the University of Toronto analyzed its $1 billion campaign (made goal: 2004), it discovered that roughly HALF the donors were first-timers. They'd NEVER given to the university before. The school basically DOUBLED its donor base in the course of one campaign.

Campaigns have the rare ability to draw new donors out of the woodwork, for a number of good marketing reasons.

Colin Wheildon's studies showed that black text on a white background is quite easy to comprehend, while white text on a black background is almost impossible to comprehend.

CHAPTER 33

Long Articles? Don't Bother.

You have to ask yourself: If people are unlikely to read a long article, why bother *writing* a long article?

And here's my quick answer, for donor newsletters: *Don't* bother. Save yourself the trouble. Channel your inner efficiency expert. Keep your articles short.

Your boss won't necessarily like the "shorter is better" rule

Shorter articles are a bitter pill for some to swallow . . . and I'm not just talking about compulsively long-winded writers.

Hospitals, environmental action groups, university research institutes and other science-based organizations sometimes assume they have an obligation—even a calling—to educate the outside world.

They have so much unique knowledge to share. There are exciting new discoveries all the time. And the issues of the day require expert commentary, "if we expect anyone to truly understand why this matters."

But . . . the assumption that your organization should (or needs to) "educate the donor" via its newsletter is a costly mistake.

Your donors are not a general audience. Your donors are a highly specific audience, selectively attentive. They like a little fresh information. But they don't need a lot of it.

They're automatically and deeply interested in one thing. It's personal. *Did I*, donors wonder, *make any difference in the world by making my gift?*

How short *is* short?

Fill most of your newsletter with briefer items in the 50–250 word range.

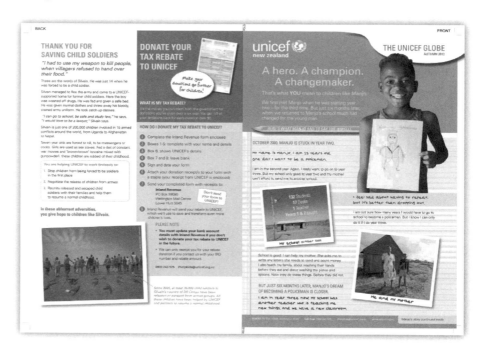

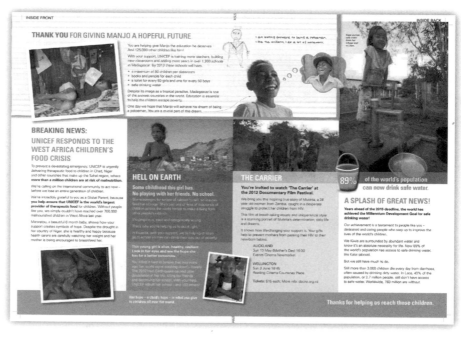

This is a high performance donor newsletter. Notice how short the articles are. Notice how often it directly addresses the reader, using the pronoun "you." The word *you* is not just a figure of speech. It is also a *profound* emotional trigger. Every time you use it, the reader instantly pays more attention. *(Reprinted with Permission)*

CHAPTER 34

Lower the Grade Level of Your Writing

Once upon a time, in my workshops, I would ask a student to read aloud a long, academic passage from a book I provided.

The passage defined two literary terms: *metonymy* and *synecdoche*. Once the students had read what I handed them, I'd ask, "So what grade level were those definitions written at? Were they written at the middle school, high school, or college level?" The consensus pegged the passage around the college level.

Reasonably enough.

But in fact—using the standard Flesch-Kincaid scale built into Microsoft Word—these highly technical, literary definitions scored at the 8th-grade level.

My point was this: you can write about anything, even arcane academic topics, at the 8th-grade level. And you should. I give you two commandments:

Write less.

Write lower.

Newspapers like *The Wall Street Journal* don't write down to their readers. They do, however, try to make their information fast and easy to absorb. On slow days, I'll check a few paragraphs from a *Wall Street Journal* feature article, just to see. Most score in the 8th- to 10th-grade range.

That thriller you bought for your airplane flight? Many will score at the 4th-grade level. Why? Because the lower the grade level, the faster you can read stuff . . . and that's what makes a "page-turner" turn.

The preceding passage, incidentally, scores at the 5th-grade level.

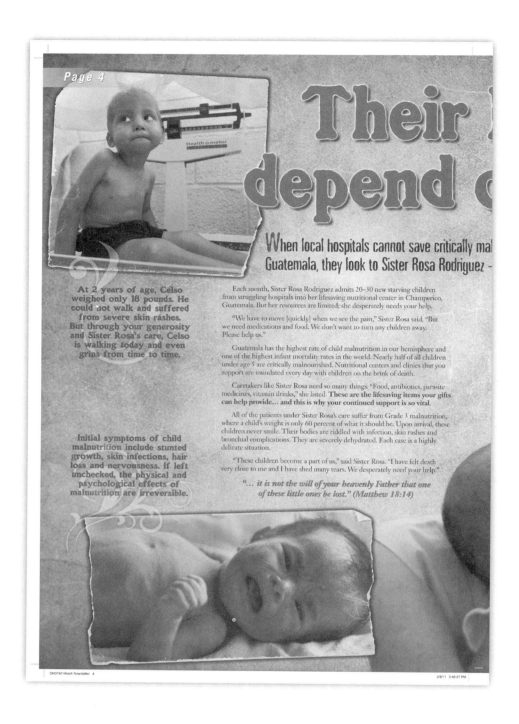

Their depend o

When local hospitals cannot save critically mal Guatemala, they look to Sister Rosa Rodriguez -

At 2 years of age, Celso weighed only 18 pounds. He could not walk and suffered from severe skin rashes. But through your generosity and Sister Rosa's care, Celso is walking today and even grins from time to time.

Initial symptoms of child malnutrition include stunted growth, skin infections, hair loss and nervousness. If left unchecked, the physical and psychological effects of malnutrition are irreversible.

Each month, Sister Rosa Rodriguez admits 20–30 new starving children from struggling hospitals into her lifesaving nutritional center in Champerico, Guatemala. But her resources are limited; she desperately needs your help.

"We have to move [quickly] when we see the pain," Sister Rosa said. "But we need medications and food. We don't want to turn any children away. Please help us."

Guatemala has the highest rate of child malnutrition in our hemisphere and one of the highest infant mortality rates in the world. Nearly half of all children under age 5 are critically malnourished. Nutritional centers and clinics that you support are inundated every day with children on the brink of death.

Caretakers like Sister Rosa need so many things. "Food, antibiotics, parasite medicines, vitamin drinks," she listed. **These are the lifesaving items your gifts can help provide… and this is why your continued support is so vital.**

All of the patients under Sister Rosa's care suffer from Grade 3 malnutrition, where a child's weight is only 60 percent of what it should be. Upon arrival, these children never smile. Their bodies are riddled with infection, skin rashes and bronchial complications. They are severely dehydrated. Each case is a highly delicate situation.

"These children become a part of us," said Sister Rosa. "I have felt death very close to me and I have shed many tears. We desperately need your help."

"… it is not the will of your heavenly Father that one of these little ones be lost." (Matthew 18:14)

r lives
on you

cally malnourished children in rural
driguez — and Sister Rosa looks to you.

Kwashiorkor is a form of malnutrition caused by severe protein deficiency. Low protein levels cause fluid retention that results in distended bellies.

Without YOU...
...innocent lives are lost.

Page 5

The headline and deck give Food for the Poor donors important work to accomplish: here, saving severely malnourished children. The articles are detailed but relatively brief (this one is fewer than 250 words long) and tend to end with a quote from the Bible, in bigger type. Living the word is part of the emotional reward for faith-based audiences. *(Reprinted with Permission)*

It's all about those ratios

The most common objection I hear, when I tell people they should write at the 8th-grade level, is this: "All my readers are college educated. They don't need the material dumbed down."

People often misunderstand the grade-level issue.

It's not a question of "dumbing down." It's a question of speeding up.

Readers want to get through your stuff as fast as possible. They have busy lives. Write much above the 8th-grade level and you'll slow them down. Ease of comprehension and grade level are directly linked. Raise your grade level and ease of comprehension slows. Lower your grade level and ease of comprehension speeds up.

It doesn't matter what vocabulary you use, by the way. Really. Feel free to use scientific terms, medical terms, economic terms, whatever suits you. What *does* matter in your writing will be the ratios: the ratio of short words to long, the ratio of short sentences to long, the ratio of short paragraphs to long. You want to strongly favor the short over the long whenever possible. The higher your ratio of short to long, the lower your grade level.

And is a dangerous word in this context. People will often take two perfectly fine short sentences and join them with an *and*, making a longer, gangly, harder to absorb sentence. Don't use *and* without good reason.

The preceding passage scores at the 6th-grade level.

How to score your grade level

There are free online grade-level checkers. You simply cut-and-paste a passage of your prose into the checker and hit a button. Voilà.

If you work in Microsoft Word, you own a built-in grammar checker. The Word grammar checker allows you to score the grade level of your prose in a matter of seconds.

When I'm writing for a client, I score the grade level of my prose obsessively, sometimes every few minutes. I consider it unacceptable to turn in text written much above the 8th-grade level. People hire me to please their readers. Low grade levels make for pleasant reading.

In my version of Word, the grammar checker is found in the Tools menu, under Spelling and Grammar. If this feature isn't working in your Word, go to your Preferences and make sure you've selected both "Check grammar with spelling" and "Show readability statistics."

The preceding passage scores at the 7th-grade level.

CHAPTER 35

Offers Wanted

Sprinkle offers across your newsletter. Offers give your donors new things to do.

Like discover: "What's it really like to be desperately poor? Sign up for our Poverty Simulation. See for yourself why it's so hard to break the cycle." (Crisis Assistance Ministry in Charlotte, NC makes this offer.)

Like grow: "You can be the mentor that changes a child's life."

Like contribute in a new way: "Join us in this special campaign to . . . ."

The dictionary defines an offer this way: "to present something for someone to accept or reject." Here are some common charity offers:

- Subscribe to an emailed newsletter. "Stay fully up to date, with our FREE . . . ."

- "You're invited" to a celebration

- "You're invited" to an *exclusive* presentation: "A handful of people will receive my personal invitation to this revealing look at . . . ."

- "You're invited" to a behind-the-scenes tour

- Discounts "if you act now" (Everyone loves a bargain. It's the "greed" emotional trigger at work.)

- Membership ("Your family membership entitles you to unlimited visits . . . .")

- Special member-only previews

- In an email: "View this wonderful, new video . . . ."

- Promoting planned giving: "Receive your free, informative brochure about charitable bequests . . . *and see how endowed funds can perpetuate your values forever.*"

- Challenge or matching gift campaigns

- "Become a monthly donor and . . . ."

- Naming opportunities in capital campaigns

- Exclusive updates from the CEO: "There is a special group of people I make sure I contact at least four times a year . . . and you're in that group." (Remember the chapter on flattery?)

- An invitation to join an exclusive society, such as the President's Circle (Ditto, the flattery thing)

Offers in newsletters: stirring the donor pot

Successful donor newsletters include offers in every issue for three reasons:

- **Offers help strengthen your bond** with that fraction of donors (10–30 percent, maybe more?) who are "truly true believers" and might want to become more involved (like, say, volunteer or take a tour).

- **Offers create a feedback channel** so donors can tell you how much they like you. (Most charities? Stay humble. I've read the research: donors are *far* more skeptical of your effectiveness than you assume. They think you're inefficient. They think you waste money. You're guilty until proven innocent in most donors' mind.)

- **Offers can seriously boost philanthropic revenue.** Not every donor supports you just once annually. Some will make multiple gifts a year; but you have to ask, in your newsletter.

Buried offers = low-to-no response

If you were omniscient and a skilled communicator . . . *and* you could see tens of thousands of nonprofit newsletters at one time . . . you'd soon detect a self-defeating habit.

Omniscient, you'd quickly notice that 95 percent + of the offers in nonprofit newsletters are made at the end of an article; an article, research shows, which very few will read in depth.

I call it the "buried offer" habit. The typical formulation: "For more information, call or email . . . ."

But is anyone listening by that point, at the end of an article? Maybe 10 percent at best? (And research says I'm being unrealistically generous.)

Assume that no one reads your articles. Treat every offer like a little ad. Make sure your offers are easy to spot and jump off the page, visually.

Road to rewards: Change your response device from passive to interactive

Interactivity has its rewards, as every top-tier marketer knows. "Interactive" in this discussion means you give your target audience a way to tell you what they think of you.

The first draft (left) of the Houston Grand Opera newsletter made two offers on the back page. But both were buried in the articles, missed by many skimmers. The version that went to press (right) makes the same two offers far more visibly, so skimmers can't miss them. *(Reprinted with Permission)*

What follows: a true-life demonstration of the gains made when a charity changed its response experience from passive to interactive.

In 2009, WPBT2, the public broadcaster in South Florida, sent out its annual appeal to current donors.

The reply device included the common "giving string"—a series of amounts the donor could choose from. The common giving string concludes with a fill-in-the-blank option labeled something like "other."

Not this time. This time, on the WPBT2 reply device, instead of "other," it said, "Surprise us!" And a big, blue circle surrounded that option, drawing the eye.

That one change in the giving string—from "other" to "surprise us"—had an extraordinary effect.

Given the opportunity to express their love of WPBT2—customarily one of the 10 most watched public television stations in the US—donors responded lustily: the average annual gift increased by almost 20 percent.

What had happened?

- By adding "surprise us," WPBT2 made its otherwise generic (hence banal) reply device into something exciting and interactive.

- By adding "surprise us," WPBT2 invited its current donors to demonstrate exactly how much they loved the programming, through the size of their gifts. And the target audience savored the opportunity.

CHAPTER 36

Donors are "Staggeringly Ignorant." That's a Good Thing By the Way.

If you *had* to choose . . . you don't, so relax . . . between *flattering* your donors and *informing* your donors, which would you choose?

Be honest. What's your newsletter up to today?

Are you trying to educate? Or are you flattering?

Guaranteed: you'll be better off financially if you choose flattery over education in your donor newsletter. Flattery drives gifts. "Donor education" doesn't. But, as I hastened to point out at the start, you really *don't* have to choose.

Flattery and education can comfortably co-exist . . . as long as you recognize which is foreground (flattery) and which is background (education).

I was once a magazine food writer. Let me indulge a food comparison.

If your newsletter were a salad, donor flattery would be the dressing. Education would be raw ingredients. Now let's be frank: the dressing makes the raw ingredients palatable for most.

Don't let the details get in the way

Charities assume that donors *want* to be well-informed. And, of course, a tiny percentage *will* want that.

But the vast majority of your donors are satisfied with an ounce of knowledge. They don't require—nor can they consume—a gallon of knowledge.

How do I know? Richard Radcliffe told me so.

Richard calls himself Dr. Death. He's based in London. He specializes in legacy fundraising. He claims to have interviewed (as of 2010) more than 16,500 donors, asking them why they made gifts. And this is what Richard told me, in passing, in a hotel outside Amsterdam: "Donors are *staggeringly* ignorant of the causes they support."

Don't jump to negative conclusions.

In fact, he did NOT mean that "staggering ignorance" was a BAD thing. *Au contraire.* He meant, "Lucky us!!!"

Because, dear fundraiser, you really *don't* have to explain all that much to get a gift. Any new donor you acquire is probably 90 percent "pre-convinced" before you make your ask. They share your non-profits' values (for instance, faith-based charities). They could benefit from improvements in their own backyards (for instance, community hospitals). They want to win the same fight you want to win (for instance, any advocacy group). And so on.

Your donors want to change the world with their contributions. Your nonprofit is simply a means to that end.

Don't let the details get in the way.

The details of how you do your wonderful work aren't really that important to donors.

Insiders dwell on processes and details, because that's what they know. Outsiders? A little detail goes a very long way. All they truly care about are your results.

CHAPTER 37

Anecdotes vs. Stats: Which Raises More Money?

Are statistics better? ("Our city has 2,700 homeless people roaming its streets.")

Or are anecdotes better? ("Meet Henry. He doesn't smell very nice. And he's ashamed of that. Because he wasn't raised that way. But it's hard to stay clean when you're homeless.")

The answer, without a doubt: anecdotes, especially anecdotes about a single person ("Meet Henry") are *much* better at raising money.

Journalists, preachers, and other professional storytellers won't be surprised. Scientists, engineers, and policy wonks will probably protest. But psychology and neuroscience say it's so.

Statistics, in fact, have the sad distinction of actually *deflating* charitable giving, according to Dan Ariely, whom I mentioned in an earlier chapter. Dr. Ariely is the James B. Duke Professor of Psychology and Behavioral Economics at Duke University and author of the New York Times bestseller, *Predictably Irrational: The Hidden Forces That Shape Our Decisions.*

In the laboratory, in a head-to-head comparison of individual donor response, anecdotal evidence (stories) raised more than twice as much as statistical evidence (numbers).

And that was only part of the problem. Dr. Ariely's research also showed that the mere *presence* of statistical evidence *significantly* lowered the average gift size.

Consider two passages, both written by Jeff Brooks:

1. There are more than 4,000 homeless and food-insecure people in our city. Most of them are women and children. On the coldest nights, all the shelters fill up, leaving many with no place to go and no food to eat.

2. The wind howls, hurling sleet into the little girl's face. She pulls her tattered sweater close around her thin shoulders. "Mommy," she whimpers, "Do we get dinner tonight?" Her mother looks down and draws her close. "I don't think so, honey," she says, quickly brushing away a tear from her cheek. "Not tonight."

The first passage is how charities typically present their case for support: with a trophy statistic (4,000) and a dash of jargon ("food-insecure").

The second passage shows how Jeff would write the very same thing. He knows his job. He's trying to bridge the "empathy gap." He's trying to grab the reader by the heart, using sensory details as his basic tool. There are no statistics. Instead, he puts the reader right into the scene, witnessing the dreadful drama of hunger first-hand.

Scientists, insiders, and policy people love the data. But numbers engage the rational part of our brain—and that part is a cheapskate, neuroscience has discovered. Stories, on the other hand, spark our empathy—and that part of our brain is where generosity proudly resides.

Requiem for a stat

Statistics are:

- Hard to understand without "translation."

- Abstract by nature (they're numbers, after all). Which makes them difficult to picture in your mind.

- Exclusive: just a few people such as program pros and other specialists understand the real implications.

- Neutral (i.e., scientific and objective).

Anecdotes, on the other hand, are:

- Understood instantly: no translation necessary.

- Concrete and specific. You can easily imagine them. They unfold like scenes.

- Inclusive: readily understood by anyone.

- Dramatic (i.e., passionate and committed).

CHAPTER 38

The Human Brain Craves Anecdotes

We're in a Golden Age for donor communications, thanks to advances in psychology and neuroscience.

Many debates are over. We've never had more information to base our ideas, offers, and words on.

We now know for sure why a bunch of hoary direct mail triggers, like flattery and fear, actually work so reliably. These emotional triggers have now been laboratory tested. We've watched the brain act in real time through MRIs. We know that flattery produces dopamine and a sense of trust for the flatterer. We know that fear tickles the amygdala, the earliest evolutionary brain bud.

We now know for sure that sad images definitely out-raise happy images, in a head to head comparison of response. That was figured out in the psychology lab. So those people who preach, "We don't want to go negative with our donors . . . ."? They're simply wrong. Science shows it.

And here's my favorite thing that science says: a taste for narrative is baked into the human brain. Again, dopamine. We take pleasure in stories. Great pleasure. Stories feel good in our brains.

Everything should tell a story: every picture, every caption, every offer, every headline, every deck, every pull quote, every testimonial and, of course, every article (but don't depend on them: as I've stressed throughout this book very few people ever read past the first or second paragraph of a longer prose piece, unless it's absolutely fascinating and probably professionally written).

A moment in honor of Rudolf Flesch

Like a lot of the things we can now take for granted because of the findings of science, the irresistible ability of narrative to lure and hold the attention of others has been known forever. Cave drawings tell stories; we're just not sure what they are.

For those of us in donor communications, it's binary:

- If you want people to listen to you, you tell stories.

- If you want people to ignore you, you lecture them with data.

I was looking at an issue of *The Wall Street Journal*. About half the front-page features that day started with a quick anecdote:

- "Elizabeth Grubesich was cooking in her bright yellow and white kitchen . . . when she got a call from her doctor. He told her the cancer drug she believed was keeping her alive would no longer be available." [The article explains how a change in marketing strategy at a large pharmaceutical company can have fatal consequences.]

- "SAVANNAH RIVER SITE, S.C.—Eight years ago, scientists using a metal rod here to probe the radioactive depths of a nuclear-waste tank saw something that shocked them: a slimy, transparent substance growing on the end of the rod." [The goop scoop? "Extremophiles," microbes that survive in super-hostile environments.]

- "In late May, a white Gulfstream IV jet with a blue stripe along its side touched down at a small airfield outside Seattle." [We're watching the first few frames of huge bribery scandal start to unfold.]

Why do anecdotes work so well to launch a story? I can think of a few good reasons:

- We like to meet new people (at least in print) and see how they behave in a situation. Anecdotes are intimate, too: we're right at the person's shoulder.

- A good anecdote dumps us into the middle of the action, at a pivotal moment in the drama.

- Anecdotes are fast and efficient. They require no translation. We understand what's going on instantly because it's all show, no tell. We watch one person or a few people do something. And in the process, we learn a lot just by observing.

Take a second look at *The Wall Street Journal* anecdotes. Note the use of concrete details to paint a picture in your mind: "cooking in her bright yellow and white kitchen," "metal rod," "a slimy, transparent substance," "a white Gulfstream IV jet with a blue stripe along its side." These details don't necessarily have news value. They don't always contribute important facts. But they do set the scene, so you can easily imagine it.

Rudolf Flesch, "the man who taught AP how to write" I've heard him called; the man behind the common readability scales I mentioned earlier, was quite clear in his revolutionary 1949 book, *The Art of Readable Writing*. "Your facts may be complete and convincing, but your reader won't remember them ten minutes afterward if you haven't bothered to [provide] specific illustrations." Like anecdotes. "Not that he will necessarily remember the illustration or anecdote itself; but it will help him remember the main idea."

What makes a successful anecdote

A good anecdote for a donor newsletter has some or all of the following characteristics. It . . .

- . . . is rich in concrete detail. At a minimum a specific time, place, and problem. Remember: details are reassuring to the reader. Details (" . . . a warm white bed in an apple green room that still smelled of fresh paint in the corners . . .") make an anecdote easy for the reader to "see" in their heads. In other words: "You are there!"

- . . . focuses intimately on a single person or a couple.

- . . . shows impact (i.e., how the donors' gifts made a direct difference in lives).

- . . . is emotional. Talks about feelings: fear, anger, loss, despair, triumph, pride, relief, hope.

- . . . is surprising, shocking. "Tell me something I don't know," all human brains beg.

- . . . is fast. Brief is fine. When the donor newsletter from an adult literacy agency, for instance, mentions that Eddie Tomasso "finally admitted to his wife that he couldn't read when he was 56 years old," that one small but dazzling anecdotal detail is all I need (combined with the knowledge that Eddie now reads just fine) to know that this organization helps people in profound ways.

CHAPTER 39

Don't Hog the Credit

An effective donor newsletter will say the following, in some fashion, every chance it can: "With your help, we accomplished worthwhile things. And with your further generous support, we can do even more. But without your help, we won't accomplish nearly as much."

Make your donors into heroes. They deserve it.

They've invested in your promise. They've trusted you with a precious resource, their money. They desperately want to believe in your capacity to change the world, thanks to them.

Donor recognition: The true meaning of (with a nod to Dale Carnegie)

What is good donor recognition?

Is it the brass plaque engraved with a donor's name? Is it a name in an annual report, listing the donor with dozens of others who have made gifts to your organization? Is it a hand-signed thank-you note from the executive director?

All of the above. And none of the above.

Recognition is really about making the donor feel—FEEL, not think—that her or his support matters deeply to your organization and the world . . . whether that support is $10 or $10,000 or $10 million.

Dale Carnegie, in his classic *How to Win Friends and Influence People* (first published in 1936 and still in print), has a lot to say about the basic human desire to feel important.

Carnegie lists eight things "every normal adult wants." These include health, food, sleep, money, sex, our children's well-being, "life in the hereafter." He adds, "But there is one longing almost as deep, almost as imperious, as the desire for food or sleep which is seldom gratified. It is what Freud calls 'the desire to be great.' It is what [American philosopher John] Dewey calls the 'desire to be important.'"

Bottom line: we want our lives to matter.

Beth Stafford, executive director of Manchester Area Conference of Churches, often tells her donors, "Do you have any idea of how important you are to the work we do?" When she reports her agency's accomplishments, the donor is placed front and center: "Could we provide over 40,000 meals to a hungry community in one year? NOT WITHOUT YOU we couldn't." Over and over she repeats this mantra. (The attentive will notice that a statistic holds pride of place in Beth's statement. And I've belabored the point that "statistics don't sell"; in fact, they can reduce response. Beth is not selling in this particular instance. She's reporting to and thanking her supporters.)

A donor newsletter is *not* about what your agency has achieved. It's about what your *donors* have achieved *through* your agency.

Tell your donors how important they are; that's the recognition they really want.

"This is YOUR victory!" an advocacy group applauds.

"Your support is essential to preserving our environment!" a conservation group reminds.

Give them a share in the credit; don't take all the credit yourself.

Show your donors that you couldn't possibly accomplish your work without them.

If you do that, they will return the compliment and support you generously for a good long time.

CHAPTER 40

What Donors Really Care About

Donors are interested basically in four things. These are kind of the "price of admission" things. In other words: do these things well, and you're on your way; do them poorly, and your newsletter won't succeed.

They are:

- **Your accomplishments.** (How effective is your organization? What did you do with my money? Are you fulfilling the mission I bought into? What are your results?)

- **Your vision.** (What would you do if I gave you more money?)

- **Recognition.** (Am I important? Did my help matter? Did I change the world?)

- **Your efficiency.** They will be surprised and delighted to hear that you spend a very small percentage of their donation on administration and fundraising costs. (You *do* point this out to them, right?)

Not to, but through

Donors don't give to your organization. They give *through* your organization to (among other things):

- **Fix a problem they worry about.** (Afraid your civil liberties are under assault in post-9/11 America? Join the American Civil Liberties Union.)

- **Sustain or expand a solution they believe in.** (Do you believe that effective sex education is a major reason why teen pregnancies are down sharply? Give to Planned Parenthood.)

- **Get more of what they like.** (Calling all bird lovers: the zoo wants to build a hummingbird aviary, the only one for a thousand miles.)

- Or (drumroll, please) **feel like they've made a difference** in their community or the world. ("My support did that? I'm so glad and proud I contributed.")

Is your organization making headway on a tough problem? Are there disturbing new trends your donors need to hear about? Are you experimenting with curious new solutions? Or bringing your proven solutions to fresh audiences?

What is your vision? What would your organization love to do if you had all the donor support in the world?

Please don't forget to say "Thank you!"

You really can't thank your donors enough. Deep, heartfelt thanks should appear in every issue of your newsletter.

Pretend you're thanking someone who's saved your life . . . and you'll be striking pretty much the right note. Your goal is to convince donors that they're critically, stupendously, IRREPLACEABLY important . . . and, furthermore, that the mission absolutely depends on their continued support.

There's another reason for getting very good at giving thanks: it's an easy way to distinguish your organization from the nonprofit mob.

Despite all the lip service paid to the importance of thanking donors, surprisingly few charities express much gratitude, experts find.

Penny Burk, in her book *Donor-Centered Fundraising*, reports that just four in ten donors say they always receive a thank-you letter after they make a donation. Lisa Sargent, an internationally respected specialist in building donor relationships, regularly conducts her own "secret shopper" tests. She sends gifts to new charities, just to see how they behave toward her. Her conclusion: "Many nonprofits [never send a letter at all.] Or they wait so long to respond that the poor donor has forgotten who they are—and the moment is lost."

It's a shame and poor practice, but it's a fact.

So take advantage of it.

Thank your donors conspicuously . . . and you *will* stand out. Thank your donors conspicuously . . . and that graciousness will become a key part of your "brand" (i.e., what they think of you). Thank your donors conspicuously . . . and they'll continue to give.

It's as basic as one plus one equals two.

CHAPTER 41

Age Matters

Why is knowing the average age of your donors keenly important? Because, obviously, 75-year-olds don't subscribe to *Teen Vogue*.

Our interests change throughout our lives. *We* change throughout our lives. Age definitely matters. You as a 20-something . . . are different from you as a 40-something . . . are different from you as a 60-something . . . are different from you as an 80-something. And not just different physically, but different emotionally.

Geriatric specialist, David Solie, author of *How to Say It to Seniors*, points out that as people age into their 70s, two issues become paramount: (1) the fight for control and (2) the search for legacy.

"To maintain control is a primary driver for the elderly," he writes, "because each day, they feel losses—of strength, health, peers, and authority—that are staggering." But there's something "equally compelling . . . on the old-age agenda—the search for a legacy." Be aware: "Every day, every hour, whether they mention it or not, the seventy-plus age group is reviewing their lives."

This intense internal life review has important implications for fundraising. Ultimately, seniors who successfully complete their life review will want, says Solie, "to be remembered for the things [they] valued most." Charities can help with that existential quest.

For instance: permanently endowed funds

A permanently endowed fund at your local community foundation is as close as most of us can come to immortality.

Endowed funds just purr on and on, forever.

The oldest endowed fund I know personally is parked at Oxford University. William of Durham's will established the endowment in 1249. Today, William's fund (he was a childless priest) stills makes scholarships possible, more than 760 years later.

Technically, that stretch of time isn't "forever."

For many, honestly, it's close enough.

See the accompanying bequest ad created by the Hampton Roads Community Foundation. It's one of a series run in the foundation's print newsletter. They've seen good results.

Who exactly are you talking to?

As the massively influential UK copywriter George Smith (1940–2012) advised, "All fundraising copy should sound like someone talking."

Not a lecture. Not an essay. Not a sales brochure. Just a talk, between two friendly people concerned about something important to the community . . . whether that "community" is local, regional, national, or international.

In order to have that conversation, you, as a writer of a newsletter, need to "see" (mentally) the person with whom you're speaking. "Try and get a fix on that individual," Smith wrote, in his *Tiny Essentials of Writing for Fundraising*. "You are talking to a real person, not a list."

Smith had one other crucial but easy-for-everyone bit of advice: "Think of your mum every time you write a piece of fundraising communication. *She is* probably the likeliest model of the average donor you will ever meet."

When I write fundraising materials, I often envision my mother-in-law, Jane. She's in her later 80s.

Is Jane's age typical? I asked a client, a large hospital system in California, to tell me what its data revealed. The hospital reported back:

- Average age of the person they *solicit* for a gift is 65 or above.

- Average age of the person who actually *gives* is 75 and above.

I asked Jeff Brooks, "What do you think is the average age of a U.S. donor?" You met Jeff earlier in this book. He has access to vast amounts of current data from direct mail appeals.

"I think saying 65 and up," he answered, "is about as accurate as possible for an across-the-board number."

Jeff did allow that the average donor's age "varies by organization and sector." But for sure: "One thing we've seen is that charitable giving as a sustained lifestyle-type activity isn't meaningfully found until around age 55. The behavior picks up steam in the following years," said Jeff, "gets truly meaningful around 65, keeps growing, then starts to drop some time after 75."

Ages 55–75: that's a 20-year window of high returns.

Jeff also noted, so you don't draw the wrong conclusion: "The drop-off at the upper end is caused by 'involuntary lapsing.'" I.e., death.

Rise of the baby boomers—yet again

You know who's just beginning to turn 65, as I write this book?

The baby boom generation: people born between 1946 and 1964, during the procreative orgy that exploded after World War Two.

In that conflict, 60 million of our species died. The subsequent natal frenzy minted 76 million new humans *in the United States alone*.

Those same newborns are now aging into their prime charitable years.

Jeff Brooks, who I cited above, had a postscript: "The smart thing to do is to increase your donors, ages 55–65. They have higher average gifts and long life expectancy, which gives them the best long-term value. If we could get all the misguided energy for finding 'young donors' aimed at this group, it would be a very good thing."

Eyes over 60

In 2012, AIGA, America's professional association for graphic designers, issued a recommendation based on research: that you use 14-point type for body copy such as articles and direct mail.

$1 Million Grants Challenge Nonprofits To Double Endowments

Two southeastern Virginia nonprofits were recently awarded $1 million endowments plus the opportunity to double them to $2 million each. Virginia Beach philanthropist Jane Batten started the permanent endowments, which are administered by the Hampton Roads Community Foundation.

Recipients are the Eastern Shore of Virginia Barrier Islands Center in Machipongo and Places and Programs for Children, which operates Children's Harbor preschool centers in Chesapeake, Norfolk, Portsmouth and Suffolk. The new endowments will provide the nonprofits permanent sources of annual funding.

Each Batten Challenge recipient has five years to raise an additional $500,000 and receive dollar-for-dollar matching funds up to $500,000. The new endowment recipients join five other Hampton Roads nonprofits that

Of The Hampton Roads
Community Foundation

previously received Batten Challenge grants. All are actively seeking matching dollars. They are: Academy of Music, Horizons Hampton Roads, Park Place School, Portsmouth Museums Foundation and Young Audiences of Virginia.

All the endowment funds were provided by the Batten Educational Achievement Fund administered by the Hampton Roads Community Foundation. Since 2003 when the late Frank Batten and his wife Jane created the donor advised fund, the Hampton Roads Community Foundation has awarded more than $14 million in Batten Challenge grants to organizations that focus on children and youth.

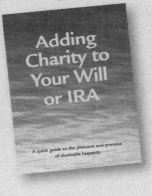
"Leave a legacy" isn't just a bunch of words. A donor leaving a charitable bequest is saying something about a lifetime of values, interests, beliefs, concerns, hopes, prayers, disappointments, regrets, mistakes, gratitude and wonder. A fund endowed by a bequest can theoretically last forever, doing good in perpetuity, in someone's name. (Or as "anonymous," if you prefer; but where's the fun in that?) The oldest endowed fund I know was established in the Middle Ages, at Oxford in 1249. It's still sending poor bright kids to university today. Editor: Sally Kirby Hartman.

CHAPTER 42

How Often Should We Mail?

The Domain Formula advises, "Mail as often as possible."
In some organizations, that'll be twice a year, given staff and resource limitations. Is that often enough? I doubt it.

Mailing a print newsletter quarterly is probably the minimum, if you want to maximize income and retention.

Look: every time you contact a donor, you make an impression, for better or worse, whether you intend it or not. When you're only in touch occasionally with news, you risk creating the impression that your organization is slumbering or fading or frail or insignificant.

And if you mail your print newsletter only once a year? That's called an annual report. Most of the charities I work with generate news and stories every day; every hour, in many cases. You just have to know where to look.

Pastor John at Community Emergency Service—mentioned earlier, in the chapter called "What a front page is for"—mailed monthly.

He'd send nothing more than a single sheet of paper printed both sides, mailed in an envelope with a reply envelope enclosed. His newsletter was the rough equivalent of a collection plate circulated by mail among the faithful. And they responded deeply.

"What would CARE do?"

In 2010, Lisa Sargent made a first gift to CARE, a global, $600+-million-a-year charity working to improve the lives of poor women and girls. She then kept a log of what she received. Newsletters play a role at two points in CARE's donor cultivation effort (look for the bold-faced items):

1. **3 weeks after her gift**, she got a "thank you" packet. The packet contained a receipt; **a special "welcome edition" of CARE's**

newsletter; and a postpaid "business reply envelope" (BRE), in case Lisa was so inspired by the welcome that she wanted to send another gift.

2. 4 weeks after her initial gift, she received a "communications preference" card. Preference cards ask each new donor to specify the communications she/he wishes to receive. Preferences might typically include: how often you'd like to receive a newsletter, how often you'd like to receive appeals, how you'd like to receive information (via emails, postal mail, or both). When organizations allow donors to control their personal "information flow," they are more likely to stay with the organization and to increase their giving, as Sargeant and Jay showed in *Building Donor Loyalty*. This preference questionnaire was the only mailing from CARE, by the way, that didn't include a reply device for making another gift. "CARE isn't shy about asking for donations," noted Lisa Sargent, "and asking repeatedly."

3. 7 weeks after her gift: She received a mail appeal making a matching gift offer.

4. 8 weeks after her gift: She received a phone call promoting monthly giving.

5. 9 weeks after her gift: She received the follow-up mailing she'd requested during the phone call.

6. 10 weeks after her gift: She received a sustainer (monthly giving) mail appeal.

7. **11 weeks after her gift**: She received a **donor newsletter**. It arrived in a envelope, enclosed with a BRE and reply device, in case she wanted to send another gift.

8. 12 weeks after her gift: She received a "giving record" mailer for her tax files, enclosed with a BRE and reply device, in case she wanted to send another gift.

CHAPTER 43

An Easy Alternative: The Newsy-Letter

Instead of always going to the time and expense of designing and printing an official-looking newsletter, try fleshing out your schedule with a less formal hybrid, the so-called "newsy-letter," as Simone Joyaux dubbed it.

The newsy-letter is the equivalent of a letter to mom. It's a chatty update. News-filled. Unstuffy. Anywhere from two to four pages long. It's not a business letter. It's not a solicitation letter (though feel free to enclose a gift envelope). It's more like a phone conversation in print. "Hey, I'm just calling to let you know about some stuff that's happening . . . ."

For example:

Dear Jane Donor,

First of all . . . let me say thank you.

This year, your gift was especially important. Let me tell you how:

The newsy-letter offers you a fast way to get something out the door to donors.

Bang it out. Don't overthink it. You're just saying hi. Talk about the organization's best accomplishments in the last few months. Talk about pressing needs or aspirations. Copiously thank the donor for his/her past contributions to your mission and vision. Sign your name. You're done.

You might be tempted to turn your newsy-letter into a solicitation letter. Caution: while it's fine to make a small ask, the point of the newsy-letter is to bear news, not to push for gifts.

CHAPTER 44

The *High Noon* Checklist

The film *High Noon* dramatized a common conflict: "personal safety" vs. "the right thing to do." The town marshal faces a gang of killers by himself, against all odds, even rejection by his wife.

We want to be heroes. Fundraisers want to do the right thing. But that's risky. Charity bosses tend to be wary. It's not what you've done before. And you really don't know if your audience will like it. *(Spoiler alert: they will; it's the way their brains are wired.)*

When you get the trembles, here's a checklist that will keep you moving in the right direction . . . .

[ ]   Is your newsletter the right length? 4–6 pages long? (**Tip:** 2 pages is too short. 8 pages is too long. 16 pages, you're just murdering innocent trees.)

[ ]   Are your key messages skimmable? Can a reader ignore the articles in your newsletter and *still* absorb key feelings and ideas? Are the headlines full-bodied? Do all the photos have captions? (**Tip:** Pretend the articles were invisible. Would the headlines do the necessary work by themselves?)

[ ]   Is there enough need? Have you given your donors problems to solve? Have you given them something important to do? (**Tip:** Balance "happy ending" stories with "need" stories.)

[ ]   Is there enough joy? Your donor is your customer. You have one thing to sell: repeated doses of dopamine (i.e., joy). (**Tip:** A reader should encounter donor-loving flattery within 1–3 seconds.)

[ ]   Are you hogging the credit? (**Tip:** Your newsletter is *not* about how *great* your organization is. Your newsletter *is* about how *great* your donors are.)

[ ] Is there at least one offer? Offers give your readers things to respond to . . . and give you an easy way to evaluate whether anyone's listening. (**Tip:** Put a coupon box around every offer. Coupon boxes reliably elevate readership 10% or more.)

[ ] Are your photos intimate enough? The bigger the face, the better; basically. (**Tip:** Siegfried Vögele in his seminal research discovered that big eyes are "reader magnets.")

[ ] Are you still trying to sell statistics? The right anecdote is a thousand times more powerful than any statistic: atomic bomb vs. firecracker powerful. (**Tip:** Collect stories, not numbers.)

[ ] Did you accurately visualize your target reader? Do you know whom you're writing to? There's good evidence that the "average donor" in the U.S. is 65 years of age or older. (**Tip:** Make references that are age-appropriate. What did they grow up with?)

A Successful Donor Newsletter Overhaul

Since early 2010, MQI — a Dublin-based charity helping Ireland's homeless and hungry for nearly half a century — has been relentless in its quest to create newsletters that are increasingly donor-driven.

From the you-focused headlines to the readable design, personal tone, and donor gratitude buffet offered on each of its four pages, the now-beloved donor newsletter is published under the genius of Merchants Quay Ireland's American-born Head of Fundraising, Denisa Casement.

Three times yearly, Casement and her fundraising manager, Nick Jones, give US-based donor communications specialist Lisa Sargent and her design cohort Sandie Collette of S. Collette Design free rein to apply every donor-delighting tactic in the book.

And donors have definitely responded:

- Between Summer and Fall of 2010, after the first newsletter overhaul, response rates nearly doubled.

- Between Summer 2010 and Fall 2012, and more fine-tuning, response rates are more than triple.

- Newsletter revenues have climbed steadily too: on average, compared to 2010, per-issue revenues have grown by more than 250%.

And now Lisa Sargent, in her own words, from an article that first appeared on Sofii.org:

Let's begin with results.

Shortly after my design colleague Sandie and I finished an overhaul of Merchants Quay Ireland's donor newsletter, I received an e-mail from MQI's Head of Fundraising that read:

> "My phone has been ringing all morning with people telling me how much they like the newsletter and giving me money. It just hit doormats yesterday."

Four weeks later, the donations from that newsletter stand at €16,000 (roughly US$21,000). Even better, those revenues will soon double – the result of a matching gift on all Christmas donations up to €50,000 (a challenge you can bet we featured prominently in the newsletter).

ROI for this newsletter, after creative, printing and mailing costs is 3:1.

Thirteen Copywriting and Design Strategies That Helped Make This Donor Newsletter Overhaul a Success

1. Choose Your Colors

One of the first things to consider is the color scheme. You'll save on costs with two-color printing, but if you can manage four-color, it's a much nicer look. (The 'after' version of MQI's newsletter is four-color.)

In considering colors for sidebars, masthead, etc., strive for harmonious colors that are also consistent with the 'feel' you want to establish. In the samples, you'll see that MQI's chief color is purple and, while this dictated the main accent color, Sandie chose a different complementary color to warm things up – in this case, gold.

2. Consider the Masthead

Here is where you see a big difference between the before and after versions. The already-established newsletter name, "Quay Times," was very difficult to read in the before version. So Sandie strived to give the name a more dominant presence – and we knew she'd been successful when donors began referring to the newsletter by name.

In fact, just by glancing at the thumbnail images at left, you can clearly see a difference in the before and after mastheads, and the ease with which the title of the newsletter is legible.

3. Add a Table of Contents

One of your jobs, in any multi-page communication, is guiding readers to the next page. . . and the next. A table of contents helps accomplish that. In this case, it's straight up at the top in the masthead, which saves space and lets people easily see what's inside without making a big deal out of it. It also gives scanners and skimmers a bite-sized summary.

4. Select Proper Font and Type Size

There is an emerging trend in print newsletters to go with a sanserif font. But we still adhere to the old rules of readability: serif font for print, and sanserif -- or sans serif -- online. This is especially true if your donors are of the 45-70 age group. They're already reaching for their cheater specs, so don't go all funky on them.

You can use sanserif sparingly in print, yes -- and we do. But for body copy, we stick with serif; the one we use in the 'after' version is among the most readable. As to type size, Sandie used 11 pt on 13, which means an 11 point type size with 13 point leading (the space between the lines).

Sidenote: beware reversed-out text. This is fine to use (again sparingly) when there's enough contrast and not a lot of copy, as you'll see on the cover page of the 'after' version; reversed-out text is notoriously tough to read in long stretches. For a fabulous primer on this, see Colin Wheildon's Type & Layout.

5. Use Photos Always

In smaller and mid-sized nonprofits, it can sometimes be a challenge to get good quality, high-resolution photos. But MQI faces a different problem: in working with those who are homeless and have addiction problems, many of the women and men they help wish to remain anonymous. For this reason there are not many full face photos, which of course are best of all, because the eyes engage.

Even so, we opt to give readers even a sideways glimpse of the real people they are helping, as opposed to a stock photo of complete strangers; it's much more authentic that way.

6. Guide the Reader

As we noted in the Table of Contents section above, one of the main jobs of any multi-page communication is to guide the reader through from page to page. But you also have to guide the reader through each article – and at the same time write for skimmers and scanners, who will never read your newsletter in its entirety.

This means:

- Headlines, instead of being cute, tell part of the story

- Deck – the intro beneath the headline – tells a little more of the story

- Body copy, if long will use subheads, and tells the full story

- Jump Heads, appear where an article is continued to another page, and usually include a piece of the headline to orient the reader

Note in the 'after' version how Sandie uses design to clearly differentiate between the head, deck and body copy. And if there are pull-quotes, they stand out too.

7. Thank the Reader and Show Accomplishments

Wherever possible, without getting too saccharine, we say thank you. Our goal here is to show the reader, through stories, testimonials, profiles and more, all the amazing things their donations are making possible . . . this, after all, is the reason you're writing.

One of the ways we accomplish this is by using a thank-you message as a built-in design element: in the headers of both inside spread and page 4 (back cover).

8. Break Up the Copy

With any newsletter, we plan for a mix of full-length articles and shorter snippets of information – bulleted points, pull-quotes, call-out boxes with bits and pieces of news, shaded areas. This, again, helps skimmers and scanners get what they need, and also adds visual interest. (You'll notice a big difference here between before and after versions.)

9. Don't Be Afraid of Numbers

You'll notice a pie chart on page 2 – we always include some form of graphic that shows how a donor's money is being wisely used. And don't be afraid to sprinkle numbers in elsewhere – in the form of statistics and percentages, for example – just be sure you explain them clearly, and always bring it 'round to the donor's role in all of it.

10. Include Inside Information

It's a hard and fast rule not to bury your readers in jargon. But I don't think you need to 'dumb everything down,' either – and in fact, there are certain cases where including jargon or technical terms can make the reader feel like an insider.

In addition to copywriting for the 'after' version, I also did some of the copywriting -- and all of the copyediting -- to MQI's 'before' version (which is the summer issue of their newsletter). Look at page 3 of that issue, "A Day in the Life of a Merchants Quay Nurse." In paragraph three, Nurse Steven Doyle talks about chronic leg ulcerations. When editing his wonderful article, I simply defined the term for the reader and shared why it was a problem, then double-checked with him to be sure it was accurate. This is one way to handle technical terms.

11. Feature Offers and Deadlines

On page 4 of the 'after' version, you'll see the challenge grant prominently featured in a call-out box, along with the 31 December deadline. This creates urgency and excitement . . . and also primes the reader for opening the direct mail piece when it arrives (it's rudimentary, true, but technically still multi-channel fundraising!).

12. Call Attention to Your Website

On the inside spread (pages 2 and 3) of the 'after' version you'll see two areas where we reference MQI's website – this in addition to the URL in the footer. On page 3, the call-out is part of the photo caption. On page 2 it's in the first bullet point, referencing MQI's Annual Review.

13. Strike a Balance

Nonprofits need to tread carefully when it comes to the overall appearance of their donor communications: not too homespun (you're professionals, after all) but not too glitzy either. Sandie sums it up, saying "You don't want the piece to look too fancy, because then a donor is thinking, 'They must've paid someone big bucks to do this.' And that leads them to think you're not making wise use of their donations. My philosophy is not to overdo it."

From the Desk of . . . Tony Geoghegan

Why 'Housing First' Holds Promise for Homeless; the Vital Role MQI Will Play

Merchants Quay Ireland has been asked to play a critical role in The Homeless Agency's reconfiguration of homeless services in the Dublin area. The Agency – a partnership body of the HSE, the four Dublin Local Authorities and the Voluntary Housing sector – was established under the Department of the Environment to eliminate homelessness and the need for people to sleep rough in the greater Dublin area.

The reconfiguration will further this strategic aim in two major ways. First will be the 'housing first' approach, with an emphasis on accommodating homeless people directly into permanent housing – with necessary supports provided to ensure the tenancy can be sustained.

Tony Geoghegan

'Housing first' marks an important move from the current situation, whereby the homeless person is first housed in emergency accommodation – either a hostel or a bed and breakfast – then moved to transitional housing and, eventually, on to permanent housing. The benefit of housing first is it minimises the disruption for the person who is homeless and also lessens the duration of the homeless episode. All of the research and international evidence indicates that the longer a person remains homeless the more difficult it is to reintegrate into permanent housing and independent living.

A second way the reconfiguration will help is with extended day support services. One of the most significant service provision gaps identified, and central to the reconfiguration, is the need to have one open access support service that will remain open into the evening time. Currently all homeless support services in the greater Dublin area close at approximately 5.00 p.m.

To address this issue the Homeless Agency have asked Merchants Quay Ireland (MQI) and Focus Ireland (FI) to develop a joint extended day support service. To this end MQI and FI are working together to develop an operational plan for the new service, which will be based in one of MQI's or FI's city centre premises and will be staffed jointly by personnel from both agencies. Our aim is to commence a pilot programme offering an extended day service from 1st July 2010.

The challenge in developing this critical service is that there are no new funds for homeless services – a result of the current economic climate – so any expansion must be funded from existing resources. As such, we look forward to working with Focus Ireland in offering the new extended hours day service. And as ever, we thank you for your generous support of Merchants Quay Ireland, helping us provide quality and accessible services for all homeless people. If you have any questions about the program, please call us on 01-524-0160.

Warm regards,

Tony Geoghegan
CEO, Merchants Quay Ireland

'Housing first' marks an important move from the current situation.

In the months ahead you may receive general mailings from us. Please know we haven't overlooked your past support: these 'batch letters' are a thrifty way to grow the work of Merchants Quay Ireland, so we can help more of those who need us. You remain a vital part of this work, and we are, as ever, so very grateful for your generosity.

2009 Where the money was spent

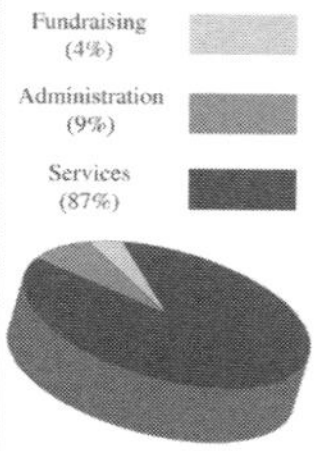

Homeless and Drugs Services
Merchants Quay Ireland
10 Newmarket
Dublin 8

Head Office: 01 524 0160
Fundraising: 01 524 0115
Volunteering: 01 524 0128
info@mqi.ie
www.mqi.ie

MQI Merchants Quay Ireland Homeless and Drugs Services

Quay Times

The Newsletter of Merchants Quay Ireland Summer 2010

MQI Merchants Quay Ireland Homeless and Drugs Services

"Something had just clicked inside me . . ."

How Marie is Winning the fight of a Lifetime

A formerly homeless mother of four is beating overwhelming odds to overcome heroin addiction – thanks to gritty determination, a deep love for her kids and the 'whatever-it-takes' spirit of Merchants Quay staff. Read about the positive changes you're helping make possible . . .

Marie loves to laugh. You'd notice that first about this pretty mom with the sparkling blue eyes. And she's not above laughing at herself, at finding humour in all she's been through. Because on her journey toward a drug-free life, Marie has learned to face both good and bad.

She's forthright about it all. The beloved horse she rode every night as a teenager, her devastation when he was sold. Out of school at 14 . . . troubles with drinking and smoking hash . . . the violence at home.

Now in her 30s, she seems to have lived a lifetime. In and out of treatment while her mother cared for her children, Marie had issues with multiple drugs – typical for heroin users – making it doubly difficult to stop using.

She hit rock-bottom before realising her true source of strength: her children. By then her mom was out of patience – the kids would always have a home, but Marie was on the streets. "She was a great supporter, and I'd be lost without her . . . I ended up homeless then and in the hostels. I used to have a photograph of me kids on the shelf and I wanted to stop taking [the drugs] but I couldn't. No pride, no dignity – everything just goes out the window. So I decided I needed to get help."

Like many of Ireland's nearly 15,000 heroin users looking to break the addiction cycle, Marie faced an uphill battle. She'd decided to seek treatment, but was still surrounded by drug users at the hostel – including a friend who smoked heroin constantly. "I used to sleep with a T shirt over me face so's not to smell it . . ."

Even at High Park, our residential treatment programme, it wasn't easy . . . especially for a woman. Of every ten drug users in treatment, just three are female. Marie explains that it's tougher for women "With children especially. I don't think I could go through treatment knowing that my kids were in someone else's house being looked after . . . it's very hard on the mothers and I can only imagine what it's like on the kids."

Marie found strength in a photo she always kept of her children.

She credits Merchant's Quay staff for helping her stay in the programme. "They sat up with me 'til one or two o'clock in the morning and if you were going through something they'd ask . . . they won't let you hide in any corner. With other places I never really got that."

Marie remembers when she'd turned the corner. It was, she recalls, "when my kids came up to see me. I just started to realise that I want to be there for my kids. From that moment on I really started putting the work in."

Today Marie is drug-free, in recovery housing and attending our aftercare sessions. She couldn't be more delighted, summing it up with customary wit: "I used to ring High Park when I left and I'd be havin' a chat with the staff and I'd say, 'I want to come back.' And they'd say, 'We miss you . . . but we don't miss you that much!' I'd be lost without the support from Merchants Quay. I'm grateful that I got the chance to go in there. Me kids they are benefitting so much from it."

For Marie, and for so many others, you are making a real difference. Thank you so much.

The Healing Hands of Sister Brid

Sister Brid O'Sullivan reflects on her life and her work as a nurse at Merchant's Quay, helping the homeless and those struggling with addiction problems in Dublin.

From the start, Sister Brid has been active as a nurse at Merchant's Quay. "My first day, I had lunch with a nurse who worked there. After lunch, there was an overdose. Somebody had collapsed. So we just grabbed the bag and went over and did CPR."

She found her calling at just 19, to the Franciscan Missionaries of the Divine Motherhood. These first years as a nun shaped her future, and Sr Brid trained as both a nurse and midwife.

Homes for the homeless. Food for the hungry. Recovery for those who are addicted to alcohol and drugs.Thanks for helping make it all possible.

In 1972 she set off to Africa.

Specialising in leprosy, Sr Brid worked as a nurse with four nuns from her Order in the swampy area near Lake Bangweulu, in Northern Zambia. There she helped upgrade the local health centre to a hospital with X-ray service, the community's first.

She recalls those years fondly, saying, "Africa was the cherry on the icing for the life I chose."

Africa was also where Sr Brid honed nursing skills that – combined with her ready smile and caring heart – would prove invaluable to Merchant's Quay Ireland, and she joined the medical staff in 2004, at our busy, Dublin-based outreach service.

Today Sister Brid sees over 300 people who turn to Merchant's Quay daily.

She's learned that their life stories of drug use, poverty, prison, loss and abuse aren't easily told. "Some stories are just so sad and very painful to listen to, so you can imagine what it's like for the clients themselves."

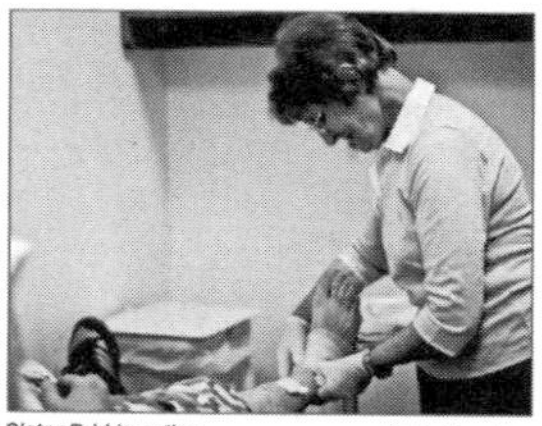

Sister Brid in action. Photo by Steven Doyle

The Merchant's Quay philosophy of respecting clients – at whatever stage they're at – is crucial, she feels, as are services offered through needle exchange and Open Access facilities, like medical care and counselling, Sunday dinners, and practical help finding a home.

But the need far outpaces present capacity, notes Sister Brid, and not just in Dublin.

"We're referring people all the time to detox and drug rehabilitation, adding their names to the waiting lists. We need far more detox services in this country. We're caught in Ireland."

Merchant's Quay provides two Residential Drug Treatment facilities in Ireland: St Francis Farm in Co. Carlow and High Park in Drumcondra, Dublin. Both have waiting lists.

A Day in the Life of a Merchants Quay Nurse

My name is Steven Doyle, and I joined Merchant's Quay as a full time Nurse back in April 2009. I work with Nurse Brid O'Sullivan – whose story you'll also find in this newsletter – and the rest of our medical team at MQI's Primary Healthcare Unit. We provide primary healthcare to people who are homeless, as well as men and women who have problems with alcohol or drug use.

As you can imagine, being homeless or having a drug problem is a challenge in itself. But a host of medical issues are related to addiction and sleeping rough, and as a Nurse, I see many of these.

I can honestly say there is never a dull moment. I might clean a wound or treat a minor injury, then see someone with an acute or chronic illness. Right now a big concern is treating chronic leg ulcerations. It's like a wound that won't heal, which is frustrating for us – and exhausting for our clients. We also test for blood-bourne viruses like Hepatitis C.

The issues are sensitive, but we always speak openly with the men and women we help – whether we're talking about safer injecting practices or the connection between healing and a healthier diet. By understanding the nature of their wounds and other illnesses, they can become an active part of the healing process.

Nurse Steven Doyle in a rare moment of quiet.

And once they feel better, many begin working toward a better quality of life.

"The issues are sensitive, but we always speak openly with the men and women we help."

I feel honoured to care for each and every one of my patients at the Merchants Quay Ireland. I can say from listening to their stories that there is a stigma around substance misuse and homelessness. But when you sit down and hear the hardships they've gone through in their lives – and still go through on a day-to-day basis – you see beyond the addiction and homelessness and the real person shines through. They are some of the gentlest, nicest people and despite all they've endured, they have so much respect for the ones who care for them.

Nurse Steven Doyle is a dedicated part of the five-member medical team at the Merchants Quay Ireland Primary Healthcare Unit. He invites you to say hello when you're next in Dublin, and see the healing work your donations make possible. To arrange a visit, call us at 01-524-0115.

How you can make a Euro *stretch* a whole lot further!

By setting up a standing order, you help us to plan more efficiently and effectively so we can help more people.

If you pay income tax through the PAYE system your monthly donation can GROW 25% - 69% when we claim tax back from the government.

Monthly € donated	20% tax bracket Your donation + tax reclaim	41% tax bracket Your donation + tax reclaim
€21	€26 (€312 yearly)	€35 (€420 yearly)
€25	€31(€372 yearly)	€42 (€504 yearly)
€42	€70 (€840 yearly)	€70 (€840 yearly)

To set up a standing order go to www.mqi.ie and download the form.
Or ring us on 01 524 0160 and we will post a form to you.

MQI donor newsletter BEFORE

Quay Times

MQI — Merchants Quay Ireland — Homeless and Drugs Services

The Newsletter for Supporters of Merchants Quay Ireland | Autumn 2010

"That Was When I Was Young and Innocent..."

Liam's story is one every parent fears. And with 15,000 people across Ireland who are caught in heroin's grip, it's all too real. Read how it's turning out, thanks to you:

"That was when I was young and innocent," Liam begins. "We used to go down to Seapoint, Dun Laoghaire baths. I used to love swimming...."

His story is one every parent fears. "I grew up too fast. Hit me teens, like. The ecstasy and smoking hash and I just tried to be part of the

> **"I wouldn't be here now if it wasn't for Merchants Quay Ireland. I'm very grateful for people who have helped out." Thank you!**
>
> Liam, pictured at left, learned new computer skills at MQI

scene ya know, experimented in trying heroin."

Heroin is one of the most addictive drugs available. In the span of 180 days, Liam was smoking heroin every day. "One day I woke up I was vomiting, shivering, bleeding. It had a hold on me."

He was injecting by 19, to a point where he "had no veins left." He robbed and was homeless for "three or four years, in and out of hostels. Being on the street definitely increased my drug use."

With nowhere to turn, he came to Merchants Quay for meals. "I used to go into the drop in-at 7.30 when they opened for breakfast, just around the corner from the needle exchange." Then a staff member helped Liam get on our Stabilisation Programme (see story below). He'd sought help before, but the

continued on page 4 >>

MQI's Stabilisation Programme:
Behind the Scenes with David and Maeve

A chat with Team Leader Maeve O'Callaghan and Assistant Supervisor David Sherry, of Merchants Quay's Stabilisation Programme.

MQI: Can you tell us about the Stabilisation Programme?

Maeve: People are chaotic sometimes when they approach us. Some of them can be homeless and looking for a space to connect in with, some can be in apartments and are sorted in that direction but not sorted in their addiction levels. Some come in from another part of the country. So before they can move in any other direction in their lives, we have to try and stabilise their drug habits, their living habits, their life skills. That's the whole point of stabilisation. It keeps them on the level – connected with us, connected with doctors,

continued on page 2 >>

Merchants Quay uses your donations wisely. See how, page 2...

www.mqi.ie

MQI donor newsletter AFTER: "My phone's been ringing all morning with . . . people giving me money."

How Will You Be Remembered?

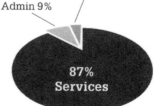

Leaving a gift in your will to Merchants Quay Ireland is a once in a lifetime chance to see that the homeless and those who struggle to overcome addiction have somewhere to turn for help, even after you're gone.

And for your kindness, we'll always remember you. To learn how easy it is to leave a legacy gift to Merchants Quay, ring Denisa on 01 524 0115.

MQI's Stabilisation Programme...

(continued from front page)

connected with any other teams to make sure they are looked after.

MQI: What life skills are they learning?

David: Well what Maeve said, the word 'structure.' The skill learned first is to get up and get somewhere; have a reason to get up in the morning. Every month there is a different programme. Life skills would be tied in with relapse prevention and say very basic maths. Some say they got involved in drugs young, and they

would have missed out on things in secondary school level. The emphasis is always on personal development. There are loads of projects, visits to art galleries, education programmes. The local employment services know we are here now. Stabilisation is a process of listening and trust and confidence building.

MQI: Are there any people that really stand out in terms of change from when they came through the door?

Maeve: Jessica (not her real name) was here nearly two, two and half years. She refused to take a chance and go outside and show what she was made of. It was a major thing for me that Jessica would be able to share the skills she had with other people. Now she has moved on to work experience and she does not want to come back. She's using the skills that she has learned, which is brilliant.

David: She even sounds different on the phone, doesn't she? It's fabulous. When you see it you say 'Wow. People can change.'

Maeve O'Callaghan, helping a client in the Stabilisation Programme

(continued from front page)

What's On at MQI?
Read All About It:

- **Just Released:** 2009 Annual Review reveals a 'rising tide of desperation' for people who are homeless; to read the review go to www.mqi.ie
- **MQI on Facebook:** Listen to client interviews and get the latest media updates on Merchants Quay's Facebook Page
- **Drug-Free Pilot Programme:** New day programme offers ongoing structure, education and counselling for clients who recently completed drug rehab
- **Scholarship Fund** to help keep education within reach for clients, page 3
- **New Aftercare House in Leixlip:** Grows capacity by 200%; provides six more places for aftercare housing and support in a drug-free environment
- **Addiction Counselling Services Contracted** by Irish Prison System: Merchants Quay to reach 1,000+ counselling hours per month in new four-year programme

How Your Donations Are Wisely Used:

Fundraising 4%
Admin 9%
87% Services

Thank you for caring.

2

www.mqi.ie

Brendan Magee Graduates...Again!

You may remember Brendan Magee from our October 2009 Newsletter. He overcame his heroin addiction by availing himself of all MQI offers – 'graduating' from a cup of tea and needle exchange to residential rehabilitation and recovery. He got a place in college, completed a Certificate in Drugs Counselling and took up work guiding others on their way to a drug-free life. Now he's graduated again, officially: he's received his Diploma in Drugs Counselling Theory and Intervention Skills. Building on this he has now taken on a full time degree course in Social Science with University College Dublin. He will graduate yet again in 2012. Well done, Brendan!

Former MQI client Brendan Magee (left) is all smiles after receiving his diploma

(To read Brendan's full story, visit 'News and Events' on our website at www.mqi.ie, then scroll down for the October 2009 Newsletter, "From Heroin Addiction to Academic Honors." Or call us, we'll post you a copy.)

Introducing the Merchants Quay Scholarship Fund

When government cuts meant less money for school and job training, MQI clients and staff were left without needed funds to continue their education. See how, with your help, a new scholarship fund is bridging the gap.

The newly established Merchants Quay Scholarship Fund will provide help with tuition fees so clients can continue their education, taking FETAC-accredited courses geared toward employment. For staff and volunteers, accredited courses must be aimed at building on-the-job skills to better help the homeless and those with addiction problems.

"With all the government funding cuts," said Denisa Casement, Merchants Quay Ireland's Head of Fundraising, "money for further education and job training is becoming harder to find. We don't want anyone who has worked hard at getting their life on track to be stalled by a lack of funding."

For more information or to donate to the Merchants Quay Scholarship Fund, ring us on 01 524 0160.

www.mqi.ie

3

A Message From Tony Geoghegan...

New Extended Day Service Helps Those With Nowhere to Go 'After Hours'

I wrote you in our spring newsletter that the Homeless Agency had identified a need for homeless services operating in the greater Dublin area during the evening time, in particular after 5pm.

In the works was a joint effort between Merchants Quay Ireland and Focus Ireland to launch a three-month pilot programme that would, for people experiencing homelessness, bring Extended Day Services to Dublin city centre.

Thanks in large part to your support of Merchants Quay, that programme is now reality.

The Extended Hours Day Service (EDS) is open from 4.00pm to 8.30pm weekdays and based in Focus Ireland's premises on Eustace Street and jointly staffed by Focus and MQI. The service is:

- Free and available to anyone regardless of age, gender or nationality
- Reaches those who need help most including rough sleepers, those without 24 hour hostel accommodation, and individuals and families in crisis
- Offers a safe place off the streets in the evenings to homeless people – the young, adults with and without children, those with and without addiction issues, and people from new communities
- Provides emergency advice, hot food, toilet facilities, needle

Tony Geoghegan

exchange, primary health care and assistance in accessing hostel.

Together with Focus Ireland, and through your kind donations, Merchants Quay are pleased to be reaching out to men, women and families who, before EDS, had nowhere to go in the evenings. We'll update you on the progress, and if you'd like a tour of EDS please ring us on 01 524 0160.

Thanks for helping make it all possible,

Tony Geoghegan
CEO, Merchants Quay Ireland

Young and Innocent...
(continued from front page)

Merchants Quay programme marked a turning point. "It put a great structure in my day. Stabilisation helped me move on from where I was."

For Liam, stabilisation meant getting referred through MQI to a safe, temporary accommodation. Eventually finding a permanent place to call home. Training courses in art, literacy, maths, and computers. "I bought a little netbook...it's only a small

computer. But before I started here I couldn't turn on a computer. Me Ma and me Da, they even say they are proud of me now."

His next step is Merchants Quay's drug-free rehabilitation programme at High Park. There's a waiting list, but he rings every Friday. "I want to learn stuff I left behind because when you are on drugs for so long, like you are blind to a lot of stuff as well," he says, then softly adds, "I wouldn't be here now if it wasn't for Merchants Quay. I'm very grateful for people who have helped out."

Coming to a mail slot near you:

Double Your Donation...
No Extra Cost to You!

Now through 31 December, your generosity doubles – and does double the good – every time you give to Merchants Quay Ireland:

A long-time supporter is generously offering a **€50,000 Challenge Grant** over the holiday season. Every euro you give this Christmas will automatically double, starting now through 31 December, up to €50,000... at no extra cost to you.

Please watch your post for more details... or give, and double your kindness, today. Thank you!

Merchants Quay Ireland
P.O. Box 11958
Dublin 8

Located at:
28 Winetavern Street
Dublin 8

Head Office: 01 524 0160
Fundraising: 01 524 0115
Volunteering: 01 524 0128

4

www.mqi.ie

Gratitude

This is my favorite part: thanking people.

I count hundreds of people as mentors: some older; some now dead; many, more all the time, younger.

Some said things to me that changed everything (Richard R., Guy M.). Some took me inside their work (Sean T., Steve T. and Mary A.). Some ran workshops that left my jaw dropped and my presumptions in smoking tatters (Mark P.). Some wrote revealing, essential books (Mal W., Jerry P., Kay G., too many to count): a special thank you, authors.

At the front of that very long mentor line is someone who did all of the above: my best friend-wife-colleague-indescribable, Simone J.

Simone and I talk about fundraising constantly, daily, nightly, on vacation. We love our life together in the charity world: there are so many different wonderful, stunning missions and methods and mad excess. And more all the time. Which is fabulous. Greed has had its day. Solving problems collectively is the future.

This book would not exist without wisdom, advice, research and examples from, among others:

Achieve Hartford!, Karen Affeld, Agents of Good, AIGA, Carolyn Appleton, Dr. Dan Ariely, Kent Ashworth, Bob Ball, Boys & Girls Club of Pawtucket, Jeff Brooks, Ken Burnett, Prof. Josiah Carberry, Dale Carnegie, Dana-Farber, Joe DiMaggio Children's Hospital, Drug Policy Alliance, William of Durham (d. 1249), Rudolf Flesch, Food for the Poor, Genesis HealthCare, Gillette Children's Specialty Healthcare, Jonathon Grapsas, GrowSmartRI, Hampton Roads Community Foundation, Houston Grand Opera, Jerry Huntsinger, Lady Bird Johnson Wildflower Center, Kerri Karvetski, John Lepp, Jen Love, Manchester Area Conference of Churches, Kivi Leroux Miller, Mark Phillips and the Bluefrog team, the late lamented print *Newsweek*, Nashville Rescue Mission, Operation Homefront, Richard Radcliffe, Adrian Sargeant, Lisa Sargent, Save the Children, Jen Shang, Sister Servants of the Blessed Sacrament, David Solie, SPANA, Christiana Stergiou, Clovis Thorn, Sean Triner, UNICEF New Zealand, Siegfried Vögele, and Colin Wheildon.

About the Author

Tom Ahern could walk into any bar in the fundraising world...and someone would buy him a drink.

He is considered one of the world's top authorities on how to make donor communications more profitable. He specializes in applying the discoveries of psychology and neuroscience to the day-to-day business of inspiring and retaining donors.

He is the author of four previous books on donor communications, all well received. Each year, he delivers dozens of workshops and webinars. Outside North America, he's spoken at the IFC in the Netherlands; several times in Australia and New Zealand; in Belgium, Italy, and Slovakia.

His recent clients for cases, direct mail, newsletters and training include Carnegie Library of Pittsburgh, Catholic Relief Services, Houston Grand Opera, the Museum of Flight (Seattle), National Parks Conservation Association, Princeton University, Save the Children, Sharp HealthCare and other major hospital systems, United Way of Anchorage, University of Chicago, Volunteers of America; as well as many smaller and local nonprofits. He collaborates with Prof. Adrian Sargeant and psychologist Jen Shang on prototyping innovative direct mail packages for PBS TV.

Tom Ahern has been an award-winning journalist, for articles on health and social justice. As a "message strategist," he's won three prestigious international IABC Gold Quill awards, all for nonprofit communications campaigns that achieved unusual success.

He graduated from Brown University with a BA and MA in English. He completed his Certificate of Advertising Art from the Rhode Island School of Design. His offices are in Rhode Island and France.

Emerson & Church
PUBLISHERS

15 Brook Street • Medfield, MA 02052
Tel. 508-359-0019 • Fax 508-359-2703
www.emersonandchurch.com